THAT REMINDS ME
OF A STORY

THAT REMINDS ME OF A STORY

JAMES GRABAU

To order additional copies of this book, contact:
Xlibris Corporation
1-888-795-4274
www.Xlibris.com
Orders@Xlibris.com
71053

CONTENTS

Dedication

I would like to dedicate this book to my parents Ray and Nettie Grabau and my incredible wife Nancy for all the love and support they have given me in good times and bad.

Jim Grabau

PROLOGUE

WHEN I CONDENSE my life down to a series of stories, it is not a simple task. I have been blessed with a wonderful life filled with "Norman Rockwell" like qualities. To many it may seem too mundane or ordinary to even put in writing, but to me it is worth writing down if only to spend time reminiscing. I will not follow a typical through the years format, but rather chapters of my life that have defined my life and made me what I am to this point.

Nancy and I were in Cabo San Lucas, Mexico, waiting for our plane to fly home when it was delayed in Dallas, because of a sleet storm there, for about six hours. We had been on this trip with members of the Master Builders of Iowa for a week in sunny Mexico. Another couple, Bob and LaRue Maddox, spent most of the six hours talking with us about almost everything. In the course of the six hours, I told many of the stories of memories of my childhood. We became good friends, and now when Bob sees me he always says," I'll bet that reminds you of a story." That is how I named these memories in this book.

I think back over my life and career and may have a few regrets, but for the most part I have been blessed more than I deserve. I have a wonderful wife, family, and now even grandchildren. Someone once said the most valuable things in a person's life are those you would not sell for any price. These include faith, family, health, friends, and many more intangible things for which no amount of money could ever buy. I thank God and those he put in my life that helped keep me on course when oftentimes I was misguided. I hope you enjoy reading this reflection of my experiences, as much as I did remembering them, and writing them down.

Jim Grabau

FAMILY

WHEN YOUR PARENTS pass away from this life and go to their reward, you are left with many questions you wish had been asked. My father was a very hard worker, a full-blooded German with a strong will and a big heart. He had a strong faith, loved his family and his work, and centered his life on these. He was part of "the greatest generation," having been through two world wars and the Great Depression, as well as the most technological changes the world has ever seen.

I look back at my life and realize it was shaped by my parents' experiences as well as mine. My grandfather died on my dad's tenth birthday, one he shared with his older brother, Theo, on the third of January. Dad also had two sisters, Lena and Josephine. He grew up in the same home I did on the north edge of Boone, Iowa, and graduated from Boone High School in 1926. He worked hard to help support his mother and family left without a bread winner at too early a time. He had fun also and always seemed to have a smile on his face and an eternal optimism that he carried to the end of his life and, I think, passed on to me.

I worked at Lawson's grocery in high school. I was helping in the produce department cleaning lettuce with the head of the produce department, Henry Hoppe. Henry looked over at me and said, "Are you a son from your dad's first wife or his second?" I said, "My dad didn't have another wife!" Henry said, "Oh yes he did, she died not too long after they were married." I went home for lunch and asked my mother if this was true, and she confirmed it. How do you reach the age of sixteen or seventeen in a small community and not know such a traumatic event? My dad had never shared this with either my sister or me because he was afraid it might cause problems in our family.

My dad had a milk route when he was young. He would get up very early, and with horse and milk wagon deliver milk and dairy products before he went to school. He used to tell me the best part of having a horse rather than a truck is the horse would move forward to each house as he delivered, and a truck couldn't do that. The horse was also easier to start on a cold morning. I now live in one of the houses that was on his route, and it still has the small port hole he put the milk through, which, at the time, was on a back porch and is now an inside family room. I still think of him putting the milk through the small door every time I look at it.

Dad's work schedule prevented him from playing too many high school sports. He did play softball after graduation, and from reading some old clippings, I could see he was very good. He also became a very good bowler and carried a 193 average. This impressed me as I bowled one year on a team and struggled to maintain a 136 average, after which I wasn't asked to bowl on the team the next year. My dad and I went bowling later in his life after a construction accident had left him with very limited use of his right arm. He was right handed, and the first five balls he bowled were gutter balls. The last five were all strikes! He did this even after not bowling for many years and using his opposite arm.

In 1929 my dad and his best friend, Fred Erbe, a son of Trinity Lutheran's pastor, took a trip from Boone to California in a Model T. This must have been right before the depression. They wrote the names of all the major stops along the way on the car's rag top. My dad kept a scrap book full of pictures of many of their experiences. I still have the book and love to look at the small black and white pictures and imagine all the adventures they must have had. Dad and Fred worked for a man in California digging irrigation ditches both by hand and tractor to be able to keep their adventure going. I don't know exactly how long they were out there, but for at least for a couple months. Their trip inspired me to go to the west coast, with my best friend Fritz Westfall, but that's another story.

My mother was a full blooded Norwegian from a small town in northeast Iowa called Kanawha. I was told she spoke Norwegian before English. She taught my sister and me some simple words and phrases, but some were not to be used in public. When asked about my heritage, I would often joke that I am half German and half Norwegian; can you tell which is which?

This is one of the stories I wish I had asked my mother about when she was alive. I was told that her mother, or my grandmother, came from Norway with her husband, an artist, and lived in Chicago. He became ill and died leaving my grandmother with two children and no means of support. My grandmother was likely frantic with concern as to how she would raise these children and answered a mail order bride ad from the paper someone showed her or told her about. More than likely this was a general ad to Norwegian men who were farmers in Iowa and needed help from women as well as companionship. I don't know if several women answered this ad or just my grandmother, but I was told this is how she and a son, Erling, and a daughter, Elfreda, were moved to Kanawha. Years later, when I stopped to say hi to my Aunt Elfreda, she showed me a beautiful painting by her father of a Norwegian schooner. Even to my untrained eye, this was not an amateur artist.

To this union my mother, Nettie Emily Larson, was born September 22, 1907. Her father was Lars Larson, and her mother was Emilia. The other brothers and sisters were Anna, Lawrence, Henry, and Ruth. They also lost a twin to Ruth at birth, named Olga. I never met some of my uncles, but my mother's favorite brother, Erling, would come to visit us on occasion. He was big at the University of Iowa and would get us season tickets to the Iowa football games in the fifties when they were Big Ten Champions and went to the Rose Bowl. My mother revered him, and if I ever disagreed with him on any issue, I was given "the look." My Aunt Elfreda would bake kringlas for me on my birthday and mail a whole shoe box to me. I became known as her "kringla boy." My Aunt Ruth was the most humorous and had a very dry sense of humor. She shared the love of antiques with my mother, and they would go antiquing together once in a while.

The story I was told is as follows: When my father was working on a job for Lippert Brothers, he met my mother and asked her out. I know very few of the details, but do know they fell in love and married September 22, my mother's birthday, in 1937, in North Platte, Nebraska. To this union was born a daughter, Emily, March 5, 1941.

From the stories I've been told, my sister was quite precocious, and that may be the source of a whole other book. I was born July 18, 1945, at a Des Moines hospital. My mother did not have an easy labor (is there such a thing?) or delivery. I was thankful that this one time, she did not take my Uncle Erlings's advice of not having another child, or there would have been no little Jimmy. My mother always wanted a red-haired, brown-eyed little boy, and her wish was half granted. My hair was strawberry blond, but my eyes were hazel. I was born before color photography, so when pictures were taken, and hand tinted, I was always given brown eyes. I was at least seventeen before my mother finally accepted the fact that my eyes weren't going to change.

The home I grew up in was the same one my father grew up in. It was, and is, an old frame house on the north side near the outskirts of Boone. It had a large front porch that Emily and I would sit out on and play games like auto bingo for colors and models. Like many siblings, my sister and I would often disagree or outright badger each other. Her door was scarred with dents from shoes I would throw at her, only to hit the door she had slammed behind her. Being four years apart, we really were fairly close and had a lot of fun as a family.

Grabau Family, Dad, Emily, Jim and Mother

I remember the Christmases and the family trips the most. It was usually just our family together for Christmas. On Christmas Eve we would always go to Trinity Lutheran Church, recite our part in the children's service, sing Silent Night, pick up our treat sack filled with an apple, orange, and whole peanuts in the shell, and then go home and try to get to sleep so we would see Santa the next morning. We sometimes ate julekage or Norwegian Christmas bread dipped in butter at least once during the season and also ate jelly cookies and spritz. Christmas morning came whatever time passed between getting to sleep and waking up, even if it was five in the morning. My poor parents wouldn't get much sleep at all. We didn't have fancy stockings, but rather my mother's discarded nylons, which worked great since they stretched to allow larger toys. One year my sister had stopped believing in Santa, but when she woke up to a new bicycle, she ran through the house shouting, "He's been here! He's been here!" and that extended her belief at least another year.

My dad bought one of the last 16mm movie cameras ever sold for home use, with a light set up so bright that you could get a tan. Movies were taken of us opening presents. My mother would still have cream on her face and would give my dad "the look" that she didn't appreciate her picture being taken. Film for these cameras was expensive, as was the developing, but we had hours of entertainment watching them. Our favorite trick was to watch people at the dinner table take food out of their mouths as my dad would play the projector backwards. When we got the movie outfit, it came with two black and white cartoons. Remember we were yet to get a TV, as my dad told us it was just a passing fad. We would watch the two cartoons over and over as long as my dad would rewind the film. When we would ride to church together, we would count the TV antennas on top of other people's homes and badger our parents to buy a TV. Emily would go up to the Doran's to watch "Animal Kingdom" because it was discussed at school. We finally got a TV when I was in the second or third grade. The first show that came on when we turned on the TV was "The Magic Window." We only received three channels, and they went to a test pattern after the 10:00 p.m. news.

The other things I remember most about our family were our road trips. I grew up at a time when most middle class families took trips by car. My dad would plan a road trip almost every summer. First it was just to Okoboji for the Master Builders of Iowa summer picnic/meeting. This was held every summer at Vacation Village on West Okoboji from a Thursday to Sunday. Dad would attend a Saturday morning meeting, but for Emily and me, it was all fun. We made friends with other contractors' kids and looked forward all year to seeing them again the next year. My best friend at the summer meetings became Nick Antone, a very bright kid from Waterloo. I knew he was bright because he had always read most of the books my mother was reading. Except for the time we were required to sleep, enforced by our parents, we were inseparable. The greatest thing about the summer meeting was everything was free, or at least we thought so. In fact all the contractors paid a registration fee, paid for their own room, and the long weekend was taken care of. Candy, pop, ice cream bars, as well as meals were all part of the deal. This was probably not the best for a somewhat hyperactive kid like me, but I didn't complain. Nick and I had a routine we would do each year so as to cram as much fun in as little time as possible. Saturday noon was the highlight of the weekend. The Queen, an excursion boat would cruise to the Vacation Village dock and blow its loud horn to signal to all wishing to ride over to Arnolds Park that the time had come. Nick and I didn't need the horn, as we were ready at least an hour earlier. The horn would blast again for any stragglers when the boat was ready to leave. Then we were off. We were told stories of special homes on the way, but our main concern was to plan how we would utilize every minute of our two hours, to maximize the fun meter. It was usually the fun house first, then bumper cars, and on and on. When we got older, new rides were put in the schedule such as the roller coaster. The first time I rode the coaster, I was sure I was going to fall out. My arms strained to hold my backside to the seat, as I would feel it lift going down the steep inclines. I was just sure I was going to fall to my death and miss the rest of the afternoon. I didn't, and the day was complete. A ride that was unique to Arnolds Park was the Tipsy House. It was just one room with a porch-like swing in the center. I think about four people could fit on the swing, two on each side. The swing was started in motion, and then the room would rotate to an upside down position. The room was made to look like a sitting room, with a floor lamp, chair, and other items, all fastened to the floor that, upon rotation, became the ceiling. A person's brain would feel like *they* were upside down, rather than the room. This was not a ride for someone with vertigo, or a light stomach. It didn't bother me, and I thought it was great fun. Suddenly we could hear the Queen's horn again telling us the two-hour adventure was over as quickly as it began. We would get an ice cream bar covered with chocolate and nuts, a park specialty, and run to get on the boat. This beautiful natural blue water lake began a lifelong love affair with water, boats, and all the activities associated with water.

Our family took some major road trips. When you live in Iowa, almost all trips take a while to get to your destination. My sister and I did the "normal" things kids do when confined to the back seat of a car for four to six hours a day on the way to wherever my dad had planned to go: we fought. We also played the typical road games such as car-color bingo, tic-tac-toe, used the magic tablet, or read. Every few miles the question was asked, "How much further?" We went to Yellowstone, Pikes Peak, Mount Rushmore, Canada, Florida, and all points in between. I remember keeping track of all the states we traveled to or through, and by the time I was in college, I had at least forty under my belt. With college, the marines, and my family, I was in every state but Idaho, Montana, and Alaska, all of which I plan to see some day.

One year we took a trip to the East coast with Washington DC and New York as our main destinations. We went to Washington first and saw the monuments and other historical places while there, but my favorite place was our hotel swimming pool. I was in about sixth grade, and remember what I said about loving the water! Our next destination was New York City. We looked through a travel book for a place to stay in the big city, and Emily's and my input was could we find a hotel with a pool? This is usually not a high priority in New York, but it was for us. My dad located a hotel in the travel book with an indoor pool. The hotel was The St. George and was located in Brooklyn. Dad called ahead, and we had a reservation. We drove towards New York and went through the Holland Tunnel. We were pulled over at a travel information center, and a black man asked where we were going. My dad was polite but somewhat indignant to the man trying to help us. Dad said, "We have reservations at the St. George Hotel and everything is just fine." The man looked up the hotel and said, "Do you realize that it is in Brooklyn?" Dad said, "Sure do. I made the reservation!" We were soon off on our way to the Brooklyn Bridge and the St. George. We crossed over to Brooklyn and found our way to the St. George. The street was so narrow two cars could barely pass each other. The area was dark with men leaning up against buildings smoking, giving the appearance of a scary movie. Dad parked the car, and we went inside to investigate. The first thing Emily and I asked to see was the pool, of course. We were sent down two flights of stairs to a dingy swimming pool area.

We had seen enough and headed for a phone to see what was available in Manhattan. My dad was able to get a reservation at the Lexington Hotel in Manhattan on Lexington Avenue. It didn't have a pool but did have much nicer accommodations. We had a great time in New York seeing the typical tourist attractions, the Empire

State Building, and the Statue of Liberty, as well as Times Square. My big purchase was a pair of "old style" longer swim trunks from Macy's, which were a big hit at the Boone pool when I got home. These trips, as well as many others, whet my appetite for many adventures throughout my life.

My sister, Emily, was my only sibling. Emily is four years older than I. She was very close to my mother, and was spoiled by my father. Dad called her "precious," and I called her some things I shouldn't have. We shared a love/hate relationship and spent a great deal of time antagonizing each other. Emily was a good student and a bit of a "brown nose" with her teachers. When I followed her in school, many of the teachers would tell me what a pleasure it was to teach her and how sweet she was.

Looking back, I think we had a good relationship for the most part. I have never denied that I was on the ornery side in my relationship with Emily. I recall my parents letting Emily have a party in junior high at our house, a rare event. I was not really invited, but it was my house, so I was there to chaperone and was not very welcome. Some of the guy friends treated me to a Coke laced with Exlax. I don't really remember getting sick, but I think it kept me out of their fun. When Emily started dating, I would open my window, directly above the driveway, where she would say "good night" to her dates. I had a flashlight to make sure all was on the up and up.

Although we grew up living together as a family, because of the age separation, Emily and I ran in different circles. When Emily went off to college at the University of Iowa, she really started treating me better, almost as if she were proud of me. This continued even when she had her first child who was first to be named Alan, after his father, Alan Munson, but soon his name was changed to Jim, and he was nicknamed "Jim-Jim," after me.

HORSES

MY YOUNGER YEARS were a little like a "Norman Rockwell painting." I was able to learn how to do a great deal of things. One of them was riding a horse. My mother was a lifelong "want to be a better rider" and for that matter, she was always trying to improve at almost everything she hadn't been given the opportunity to learn as a child. I think this was great for me because I learned how to do all kinds of things. I may not have been the very best at all of them, but good enough to have fun and not be afraid. Horseback riding was one of them.

Our family would go for trail rides at a "dude" ranch called the AA-S, located between Boone and Ogden. The ranch was named after Art and Agnes Skone, who owned the beautiful timber ground directly above the Des Moines River. I still remember the names of many of the horses we would ride when we were there: Lady, Snicker, Dapples, and Flicka, to name a few. Each had a personality, and the Skones would try to match riders with the horse they felt matched the experience level of the person. This is how I recall my first experience with horses. I soon became more comfortable on a horse and soon felt I was one with the horse.

The Skones not only gave trail rides, but also ran a summer camp for both boys and girls. My first camp experience had been at the YMCA camp, also by the Des Moines River. I was between first and second grades and kind of a big baby. I had never been away from home, and being taken to the Y camp made me very homesick. I pleaded with my parents over the phone to come and get me, but they wisely refused. It was, and still is a great camp, but I struggled with that "vundt" feeling all week long. Making me stick it out was the best thing my parents ever did to help me grow up. When I got home, all I remembered was how much fun I had. The next summer I went to the AA-S and wasn't home sick at all, and didn't even want to go home when my week was over.

The activities on the ranch consisted of much more than just riding. We learned how to take care of the horses, swim, clean our bunk house, and our plates. The bunk house was an old school bus with bunk beds on both sides of a narrow isle from front to back. We learned how to saddle the horses, ride steep trails, groom, and get along with everyone. What a great experience my parents provided me with at a fairly young age. The Skones were good Christian people and provided great role models to all their campers. Fritz Westfall, my best friend, as well as Rick Erickson and myself, went to the camp for several summers.

A story comes to mind of one summer the Skones wanted to take a vacation from the "ranch" and go on a trip. It was after the regular camping season, so all they needed was someone to care for the horses, and lead an occasional trail ride if some group called to reserve one. Their trip was to be two weeks long, and because the Westfalls and the Grabaus had been out there so much, we were asked to stay at the ranch and keep an eye on things. One day a group came out for a trail ride that our sisters, Emily and Nancy, would lead. They would be at the front and back to make sure all went well and safely. Fritz and I had our own plans. We saddled up what we thought were the "fastest" horses and headed to the area called the cantering strip to hide in the bushes. Trail rides consisted mostly of walking the horses head-to-tail up and down hills with a few areas to trot, and the really exciting part was the cantering strip. The horses were so "programmed" they knew exactly when to do whatever was called for in certain areas. Most of the riders that come for trail rides are at best novices, and at worst, beginners, or first-timers on a horse. They used the horn to hold tight and hoped they would not fall off. Fritz and I waited patiently in the bushes for the group to arrive. Just as they started down the cantering stretch, we came out from behind the bushes at a full gallop, whooping and hollering as loud as we could. The trail riders were treated to the most terrifying ride of their lives. Sounds of horses farting, shoes being thrown, and screams could be heard for miles. We, of course, thought it was great fun and nearly fell off the horses laughing as we rode off in to the sunset. Our sisters didn't think it was quite so funny, and we were in major trouble when our parents found out. It was worth it, and what a great memory! I don't think people were into suing as much as they are today.

I don't remember the exact year my dad started looking for a horse of our own. I must have been in the third or fourth grade at the time. Tony was the first horse my dad purchased. He was a sorrel color and large-boned, like a small work horse. Dad was a general contractor with an office and shop directly behind our house, a hundred feet or so. He had his men create a barn for Tony out of the back twenty-five feet of a storage area in the red tile masonry building. It wasn't too long after we got Tony that dad bought a quarter horse mare called Babe. Chuck Parker, a friend of my dad, had brought Babe in from someplace out West. Tony was easy to catch, but not Babe. When we first got Babe, we had my dad, me, and several of his men in the clover field chasing Babe for my first ride. We were having no luck in keeping her in a corner long enough to put a bridle on her. A girl by the name of Janice Vogler lived a few miles north of our place, and dad knew she was good with horses. He called her and asked if she could help catch Babe. She agreed and was there in a few minutes. We were all amazed how she was able to walk right up to Babe and put on her bridle.

My first ride on Babe was one to remember. Babe had been trained to work cattle and was also very fast. I now thought I knew everything about horses, having stayed at the AA-S ranch and ridden most of their "nags." I grabbed a hold of the horn, threw my leg over the saddle, and started to ride. I was much like a kid with a new car taking it slowly at first to get the feel, and then I just had to see what she "had." I gave her a kick with my heels of my cowboy boots and started instantly into a gallop. This horse could run, not like Tony, the small work horse. Soon we were flying through the clover with the wind in our face and Babe's ears laid back as if to say, "You want to see me run, do you?" Things were going great when I thought I would try the brakes. I pulled back on the reins just a little, not realizing Babe and most quarter horses were trained to stop on a dime. I wasn't ready for her legs to be planted and the sudden bounce to a dead stop. I flew over the horn, Babe's head, and head first into the clover. Fortunately the clover was deep enough to break my fall, and I wasn't hurt at all. I learned that when on Babe, if you pull on the reins, you had better be ready to stop.

My mother rode Babe, too, but much more conservatively than I. She would hold on to the horn and ride much slower. I look back and realize her courage for being willing to try so many things she had, with little background or training. I was not the most thoughtful at getting gifts for her birthday, or other special occasions, so I would often, at the last minute, write a certificate for horseback riding lessons and give it to her.

Mother on Babe, Jim on Streak

When I was growing up in the fifties and TV was just becoming vogue, it was the era of great western stars such as Roy Rogers and the Lone Ranger, to name a couple. I used to love to watch them, and then play like I was in the episode I had just watched. I could jump on my horse and pretend that I was chasing the bad guys, just like on TV. I would also ride to the corner of Twenty-Second and Linn, which was a quarter mile south of our home, and wait for a car to turn north. Just as they turned, I would put Babe into high gear and race the car for as long as Babe could keep up. Most drivers would drive the same speed as she was running and yell out the window the speed we were going. It was usually about thirty-seven, which is really flying when you are on a horse. I had no fear and totally trusted the horse and my ability to stay in the saddle. To this day I still can remember the exhilarating feeling I got when Babe was running at full gallop with me on her back. I used to race anyone willing. Bob Lebo would go to his grandparents and ride a Pinto from where they lived north of me about four miles to our place, or we would meet half way. On some occasions I would talk him into racing. His horse was very quick, and the two would stretch their necks as far as possible to try to stay ahead. He would usually beat me by about a foot in a quarter mile race. There weren't too many horses that would beat Babe, but Bob's pinto was just a little faster. It was hard to get Bob to race because he always had a long ride home after we rode together. Fritz Westfall also got his own horse, but he lived in town and had to rent a place to keep his horse in the country. I do recall him riding out to see me at my home once so we could ride together. I, of course, had to challenge him to a race. We lined up facing south toward town and were ready to get the race started. We took off in a full gallop towards Twenty-Second Street, which was to be the finish line. Fritz's horse didn't stop like Babe; in fact, it didn't stop at all! It went right over Twenty-Second and just kept running. I followed to see if I could help. We ran all the way to Lowell Elementary, about five blocks, before Fritz could stop the crazy horse. I'm not sure who won, but it was fortunate that no one was hurt, including the horses!

My dad had Babe bred to have a colt. I would go out every morning to see if the colt had been born as it came closer to the time she was due. I can still remember the excitement the morning I went out to the barn yard and saw an extra four legs behind Babe. The new colt was a palomino and almost white at birth. I just knew this horse would be even faster than Babe, so I named him Streak for his future speed and a white streak on his forehead. Well, at least the forehead came true. Babe was very protective of her foal and would lay her ears back if Tony got too close. Streak was to be my horse, and I could hardly wait for the colt to be ready to ride.

We took Streak to a trainer to break him and get him to neck rein, etc. It wasn't too long before we went to pick him up to see what he had learned. I, of course, expected a similar ride as Babe, but this was not the case. Streak was a little lazy, and it took a lot more effort to get him to run. The trainer even had me wear spurs to encourage Streak a little more aggressively. What Streak lacked in speed, he made up for in looks. A palomino gets darker as it gets older, and in the late spring becomes a beautiful golden brown. I now could even go riding with my mother, which we did many times. I never was able to race with Streak, but I found out several years after we sold Streak that he became a very good barrel racer. Babe could have been good at barrels, too, if she hadn't been so spooky. She was scared of her own shadow and would not go close to the barrels.

I would guess the horses led to my love affair with two-wheeled vehicles, but that's another story. I never showed horses, but have great memories of my experiences with horses. There were three boys that lived just a little less than a quarter mile south of our place. Doug was the oldest, being two years older than I. Steve was two years younger, and Mark a couple of years younger yet. I became like their adopted brother, and we spent a lot of time together. Steve and I were the closest, but all four of us played together. They also had a horse, as well as other livestock, on their small farm. I would help them with chores because the sooner they were done, the sooner we could play. We would feed hogs, cattle, and even clean out the barn. They used to say their horse would beat Babe if it had a better rider. Steve and I used to ride up and down the ditches picking up pop bottles and putting them in gunny sacks. We would ride to a corner filling station to cash them in for the two cents apiece, so we could buy a candy bar and a pop for ourselves. Fred Graham owned the little station at the corner of Twenty-Second and Linn. Fred would sell us a candy bar for a nickel and a bottle of pop for ten cents, which included two cents for the bottle. What a deal! We thought we were walking in tall cotton.

I didn't ride as much in the winter, but I do remember having friends out to ride on a toboggan that I had been given for Christmas as I pulled it behind Babe. I would take a long rope, tie it to the thick roping saddle horn, and race across the snow as fast as Babe could run with the sled. I would then make a sharp turn and the sled would accelerate, throwing all my friends off into the snow. It was a little like "crack the whip," a game we played at the ice skating pond.

One other story I remember happened much later in my life, when looking for a horse for my daughter. Alison had also gone to a "dude" ranch near St. Charles and developed a love for horses. She was working hard at a paper route to save money to buy a horse. I had looked all over for a nice, gentle horse for her. A friend of mine told me his dad had been given a really nice quarter horse that might work for Alison. I first went to the farm with my dad and didn't take Alison. He had a saddle on the horse that was ready to ride. I rode the horse a short while, and I wasn't that fond of his gait, but he seemed to be gentle. My dad suggested that I have Doug Gustafson, my former neighbor and now a veterinarian, look at the horse to make sure he was "sound." I thought this was a good idea and told the owner we would be back to make a final decision.

Doug and I returned a few days later to relook at the horse. My friend's dad was Ray Lansing, and he had the horse all saddled up and ready for me to ride again. Doug told Ray that I could ride anything. I got up on the saddle and noticed the horse had a hackamore bridle without a bit in his mouth, and just as soon as I was in the saddle, the horse headed for the other side of the barn. Ray and Doug couldn't see the horse and me, but they could hear the sound of a horse bucking, farting, and in total control of me. Without a bit in the horse's mouth, I had no control over the horse. I looked around, and the barn yard was full of disks, barb wire, and other dangerous items. The horse came up to a fence and stopped just long enough for me to slide off. Ray and Doug were laughing hysterically. I made a quick decision that this was not the horse for Alison. A few weeks later I did locate a horse for Alison named Buffy; she was no speed demon, but Alison had a lot of fun on her.

First Day of School, Emily and Jim

SCHOOLS

I STARTED SCHOOL at Trinity Lutheran Parochial School. My kindergarten teacher was Mrs. Lippert. She was very nice and exactly what I imagined her to be. I was only at Trinity for two years when my mother thought they should or should not be teaching phonics, and I was moved to a public school. I was on a bus route, and the bus took me to Page school. I didn't know anyone there and was a little "vundt" every morning. John Doran, a nearby neighbor, befriended me and helped me get over this feeling every morning before school started.

Page was an older school that had two floors. The first day I went to Page I did not realize that the boys and girls were segregated for recess. The boys went out on one side of the school and the girls on the other. My first day I ended up on the girls' side with one other misguided boy named Oscar. I couldn't understand where all the boys went. The next recess I figured it out and went out the right door. I was only at Page for two years because the bus route changed. I had Miss Thompson and Mrs. Krigger for second and third grades respectively. I did manage to make some friends at Page during the short time I was there. The one thing that sticks out in my mind was that when we played out in the snow and got our trousers wet from the snow, we had to go to the boiler room, take them off down to our long johns and dry them before we were allowed back in class. This may explain my slow academic progress as I spent a great deal of time in the boiler room. I was then moved to the old high school building called Washington, again because of a changed bus route. Before I left my class of thirty-two, I picked up one of the jingles kids make up about teachers. There was a fourth grade teacher a bit on the crabby side, and the kids would say, "Old Miss Pence sitting on a fence trying to make a dollar out of fifteen cents." It is funny how you remember things like that and forget the things that would be more beneficial.

I was only at the old Washington for a few months, and we were sent to the old Franklin, which later became the Junior College. I finally settled for the rest of my fourth grade at the brand new Franklin School, just finished on the north side on Crawford Street. This was the first school with a hot lunch program, a program Trinity had for years. I remember a really neat feature at the new Franklin, which was the fold down lunch tables that were in the gym and, after lunch, would go back up into the walls for better utilization of space.

I didn't realize it at the time but looking back I can see they tore down every school I attended shortly after I left. I really don't think it had anything thing to do with me but it happened just the same. The only school that survived was the old Franklin that as I mentioned was turned into the Boone Junior College. I later attended and received my Associate of Arts degree from Boone Junior College. They then tore it down.

After grade school I went to the Boone Junior-Senior High School. Looking back I often wish I had been a more dedicated student. I had a lot of fun and made some good friends. I often think another year of maturity might have served me well both academically and athletically. Another year to mature might have made me a better student and athlete, but then some really good things that happened in my life may not have happened. You don't get "do over's" in life, so you have to make the best with the cards God deals you. I guess we all have things we wished we had done better, but all and all I have few regrets and look back on my life as very blessed.

I mentioned that I was able to do a lot of different things while growing up. One of these was ice skating. I was given my first pair of skates at about the age of seven or so. They were hockey skates, and I always wanted a pair of figure skates. What a difference they made. I actually became a pretty good skater. I almost lived at the skating pond in the winter of junior high. We would play "pom pom pull away," "tag,""crack the whip," and even "comedy baseball." Boone had a "movie set" skating pond with a warming house and hot chocolate. Honey Creek flowed into the man-made pond, and sometimes you could skate up the creek below arched trees covered with snow that looked like a winter wonderland. Once in a while someone would fall in a soft spot in the creek and go home with wet trousers. In junior high no one could drive, so if you could get a girl to skate up the creek, it was the next best thing to a date. We had a lot of good, healthy fun. In the warming house was a sign that read, "Why break it up? Your folks paid for it." I used to change the saying to "Why break it up? My dad built it," because Grabau Construction built it. We even played some hockey, but most of us just used sticks we found that looked like real hockey sticks rather than the real thing. Winter was not the time to be a "couch potato," but rather a time to get out and enjoy the outdoors.

We also did a great deal of sledding. I was given a flexible flyer for Christmas one year and put it to good use. My dad told me he always wanted a sled that had the grooved runners like mine, but didn't get one because they were more expensive. He still had his old sled, and we used to pull it behind Babe because it was higher off the ground than mine. We would go sledding with a friend of mine, named Skip Spencer, who lived out near some timber ground. We would name some of our runs with trees we had to avoid, names like "bloody alley" and "death's run," just to make it seem even scarier. I later received a toboggan for another Christmas and had some great times with junior high group dates. We would get together on a day when, because of snow, school had been called off. Our group would usually consist of John Bush, Pam Gustafson, Tom Anderson, Jackie Reinhart, Rick Houser, Karol Hubby, and me. Sometimes there would be more and sometimes less. We would usually walk to the area we thought would be a good sledding hill. We were then in eighth or ninth grade with no drivers license and the event was more about getting together than the sledding. These were also the times I would have the "gang" out to my house and pull the toboggan behind the horse. My mother would make hot chocolate for us and homemade cookies. This was my first experience of any type of dating. In grade school I would look at a girl I thought was cute, but I never thought girls would like me. In junior high I gained confidence when someone told me that a girl liked me, wow!

I can remember going to a school dance at the cafeteria. I was dressed in a new corduroy suit with vest and all. I felt pretty "kool." There was a boy a year older than I, and I idolized him. He had on the same suit so I would try to act like he did. I can remember my dad saying not to copy someone's actions because you usually copy the wrong things. This was good advice because this boy became a heavy drinker later, got a girl pregnant, and was killed on a motorcycle, all before the age of twenty two. The "twist" was a dance that came out when we were in school, and we all looked like nerds trying to do it. One night at "grid," a dance held at the YMCA after football games, this same boy was there and did the "twist." I thought the way he danced was really "kool," so I worked on this style at home until I was comfortable doing the dance in public.

Boone had a number of unique eating spots when I was growing up. They didn't seem so unique at the time because every town had its own variety of restaurants before the "chain" fast food places took over all cities so all communities look somewhat alike. There were several that I really miss and, looking back, really enjoyed. They weren't high end, but the food was good, in my opinion. Places like The Coney Island, Tip Top, Lincoln Restaurant; all with featured items

I now miss. We also had a great ice cream spot by the name of Boyd's Dairy that made malts to die for. They made them with special malt mixers that don't seem to be available today. I used to walk to Boyd's and call for a ride home after school events, and while I waited, eat a malt and consume an entire package of Archway black walnut cookies, talk about rich! I didn't have a weight problem because of genes and hyperactivity. There were other spots that made your home town uniquely yours; these included retail stores, gas stations, and the like, that have, for the most part, lost out in today's age of large corporations and chain stores.

I digress a lot when I think back at the years I spent growing up in Boone. Some kids can't wait to grow up and "get out of Dodge," but I look back at a really great childhood. My school years went pretty fast in junior high, and before I knew it, I was a sophomore and almost sixteen. I had a July birthday, so I couldn't drive legally until the summer before my junior year. We always made friends with some upperclassman who had a license and would let us hitch a ride with them. I received a good education at Boone High School. I took a course in physics that had a really unusual instructor. His name was Mr. H. L. Cunningham. He had even taught my dad back in 1926. The students in his class would have to get up and do a problem on the blackboard in front of the class. When you did the problem correct, you were the smartest person in the world. When you were wrong, the whole class made fun of you. A friend of mine named Rick Ericson would lead H. L. by saying things like, "Grabau doesn't know his inertia. He is going to get killed on the curve near

Jordan." H. L. would then repeat what Erickson had said. Erickson would then say, "Why Grabau is like a bear lost in the woods." H. L. would again repeat the same thing. This would go on for several minutes until H. L. realized he was being led, and then he would say, "That's enough, Erickson."

The class was tough, but H. L. was very interesting, and we learned a lot. Students could come in early to get extra credit, doing experiments. I needed all the help I could get, so I was there almost every morning. You could also get an extra point if you brought in a picture of a former student who had become successful. Fritz Westfall brought in a picture of his dad, who had taken H. L.'s class, and Fritz got an extra point because his dad was now a doctor; no questions asked. I knew my dad had also taken physics, so I brought in his picture. H. L. said, "Are you sure I had your dad in my class?" I said, "Oh yes, sir. He couldn't have become a successful contractor without your physics class. "After a great deal of talking and "sucking up," I finally convinced him my dad had been in his class. Part of the problem was that my dad was only about four or five years younger than H. L., and he had had him in class when H. L. just graduated from college.

H. L. used to fix TVs to make a little extra money. He would tell the story of some lady that would call him up to come over and fix her TV. When he arrived he would notice that it had been unplugged. He would check all the tubes, wires, etc. then plug it in and charge her fifteen dollars. He thought this was really funny. H. L. was also an avid golfer. He said, "All you needed to know about golf was the angle of incidence is equal to the angle of reflection." I think of that every time I'm out golfing and hit an errant shot. This is also true for tennis, and yet my game is a long way from perfect in that sport, too.

I graduated from Boone High School in 1963 at the age of seventeen. I was nearly six foot tall and weighed in at one hundred sixty pounds. I needed to mature academically, so I enrolled at the Boone Junior College for the fall semester. This may not have been as "kool" as going to a four year school, but I had seen many students do it in reverse, and I was smart enough to know I didn't want to come back and start over. I returned to my old Franklin school for my first semester of college. I really enjoyed my first year and met some new friends as well as many old friends that had chosen the same route I did.

I remember being at the JC when on a cold November day, I heard the sad news that President John F. Kennedy had been shot and killed. The next four days I was glued to the TV to see and hear all the news about the assassination. It was a sad day for America, and we couldn't believe this could happen in this day and age.

My sophomore year was fairly uneventful. I gained some leadership experience by being elected president of the Young Republicans. I really wasn't that politically active, but looked at it as a challenge and also a social opportunity. We recruited many members by saying we would have some good parties. We had members that were also in the Young Democrats, but they didn't want to miss a good time. Our club won an award at the state convention for having over ten percent of the school in our club. Grinnell College was the only other school to receive this distinction. This was a tough year to be a Republican. The Republican candidate for president was Barry Goldwater. He was very conservative, but had an uphill battle with Lyndon Johnson, the incumbent after Kennedy's assassination. Ronald Reagan was a spokesperson for Barry Goldwater and even wrote a book about his conservative philosophy. This was his start in politics, and I will always remember how articulate he was.

The JC had a dance in the fall called the Blue & White Formal. It wasn't a formal, but the school did nominate four girls and four guys to be "Miss & Mr. Boone J. C. I was put up and had to be interviewed by a selection committee. I remember one of the questions asked was if the voting age should be lowered. I think my answer was if you are old enough to fight, you should be old enough to vote. I don't know why, but I was selected, along with Marj Kobaldt.

I received my associate of arts degree, which was at least a stepping stone to my four-year degree. I applied at the University of Iowa and was accepted, but thought I would take a look at Texas Christian University, also since Fritz Westfall had transferred there from Iowa State. There were a number of Boone kids that had gone down to TCU for their post high school education. Dick Hamilton, who was a year older than my sister, was one of the first that I was aware of. In the spring of 1965, I took a trip to Fort Worth to visit Fritz and look at TCU. This was also my first flight on a commercial airline. I can remember the great feeling I got when the jet accelerated down the runway to take off. In a short two hours I was in Fort Worth being picked up by Fritz. It was spring in Texas, and we even went water skiing at a fraternity party that we went to. I didn't make a long, calculated decision when deciding to go to TCU, but the weather was good, the people nice, and the school seemed like a good choice.

I worked for my dad's construction company both summers between my freshman year and my sophomore year of college. The fall of 1965, I packed up my car and headed for Texas. I remember my folks were kind of teary-eyed when we said our goodbyes. I didn't realize what it felt like until years later when I had to say goodbye to my own kids when they left home for college.

I think it was a good decision to get a ways away from home to finish my degree. It made me grow up, meet new and different people, and stretch my boundaries. When I arrived after a twelve-hour drive, I checked in to the Pete Wright dorm, called Fritz, and also signed up for "rush." I was on the tennis court just practicing serves when a guy by the name of Roy Dale Ferguson stopped and introduced himself. He asked if would like to go to a pre-rush gathering that evening? I said sure I would, and that was my first introduction to the Delts.

I went through rush and met a lot of nice guys. I did end up pledging Delta Tau Delta for a number of reasons. I felt I fit in well with these guys. They also seemed to have a lot of campus leaders that I met and read about in their brochure. The final reason, and one of the most pressing, was they had room in the house for two pledges to live, and the Pete Wright dorm where I was living was not air conditioned. Fort Worth was, and is, one very hot spot in the spring, summer, and fall.

Pledgeship is a little like being a slave to the actives in the fraternity. This was worse when you lived in the frat house and were so available twenty-four-seven. My roommate was Steve Allison, who was from California. We spent a great deal of time shining shoes or cleaning actives' rooms and various other slave-like duties. We called all actives with the title MR. and had to memorize all their names. Probably because I was a junior, I was nominated as the president of our pledge class and was elected. I didn't know much about running a meeting, but after a few embarrassing times, I caught on. This served me well later in life.

The pledge class was comprised of about twenty-two guys who were mostly freshmen and a few guys that didn't make their grades the year before. The actives would plan activities to make us bond as a pledge class. I think it was on a Saturday night at about 10:00, we were gathered together and been given a list of items we were to locate on a scavenger hunt before 8:00 the next morning. I tried to organize the pledges in groups to involve everyone and also accomplish our tasks. One of the pledges was a boy by the name of Richard. He hadn't bonded very well yet with the group, so I thought I would assign him to be a driver and use his car as one of many cars needed to cover the city. "Richard," I said, "We will use your car as one of the vehicles and three guys can go with you." Richard said back to me, "I don't want to use my car; it might get dirty." Richard made it through the night as a pledge brother, but it wasn't long before the actives could see he wasn't very well accepted by the rest of the pledges, and he was black balled.

The scavenger hunt didn't have your run of the mill items on it. A few of the items I remember included such things as ten pounds of elephant manure, fifteen feet of stringed sheep manure, and a signed panty of each sorority's president, to name a few. We had guys climbing over the Fort Worth Zoo fence in the middle of the night to visit the elephant pen. One pledge brother spent most of the night in the back of a station wagon stringing sheep shit. We also had to get a picture of the pledge class with the Will Rogers' statue as soon as it was light enough in the morning, so we could have everything back to the house by eight a.m. It was a crazy night, but we had a lot of fun and did some major bonding.

The semester went by fast, with some great parties, nasty rallies, hell week, and finals. The one thing our pledge class didn't do a very good job with was study. Only nine of us made our grades to become active. This was a failure on my part as pledge president and also the actives for not putting more emphasis on academics. Those of us that made our grades were relieved, but a lot of our pledge brothers were left behind. Some transferred to other schools, and some just went on probation for a semester.

The next semester I was given the job of House Manager. This wasn't the most prestigious job, but it was some responsibility, and I tried to do a good job. I had been voted best pledge my first semester and got my name on a little plaque in the study. I probably won the best pledge title because I did really dumb things like consume ten raw eggs the actives fed me while laying on the floor below a urinal an active would stand on to bombardier me. We did a number of dumb things to prove our worthiness to become a full fledged member of Delta Tau Delta. I mentioned I was a second semester junior, didn't I? I should have been a little smarter, but instead was too "gung ho."

The second semester I had more fun than I should have. I would ask different girls out to parties we had almost every weekend. The boy-girl ratio at TCU was three-to-one in favor of the boys, so it wasn't too hard to find a date even for an Iowa boy. I was at the airport waiting student standby at Easter break, when, after missing several planes, I noticed a TCU girl who had dated one of my fraternity brothers. We started talking, and I asked if she would like to get something to eat before our next opportunity to catch a flight. I was not feeling the best and found out later I had a 102 degree fever. Between the other missed flights, I had gone to the car and turned on the heater and lay down and shivered.

Nancy Higley was the girl's name, and she was a senior Pi Phi at TCU. Being the big spender I was, I took her to McDonalds for a sandwich. We then went by her house and back to the airport.

The airport was called Love Field; could this be a sign of things to come? We finally made the next flight to Kansas City, Missouri, where Nancy was to meet her grandmother at the old airport near downtown. I had to change planes and go on to Des Moines, Iowa. I was introduced to Nancy's grandmother before I flew to Iowa. Later I was told her grandmother liked me and asked Nancy why she didn't date someone like me.

In Iowa I went to the doctor and was given a prescription to help me get over my cold, flu, or whatever I had. It was at the doctor's I found I had a fever, but I got over it quickly. Soon I was back in Texas for the rest of my junior year. I got a call from Nancy soon after I returned to TCU asking if I would like to go to the Pi Phi formal. I accepted, and it later became the best decision I ever made. I will tell more about Nancy and our romance in another chapter called Nancy.

I finished the semester, signed up for summer school, and thought I would take a history course and a foreign language, which I needed to fulfill to graduate. The history went fine, but signing up for German in summer school was a big mistake. The first thing the instructor said was, "This is a difficult language to learn in a regular semester and is very difficult in summer school." It didn't take long for me to realize that to take German was a mistake for me. I dropped it before I got a really bad grade.

The summer was filled with a great deal of water skiing and dates with Nancy. It was the best summer I can remember to that point of my life. I had a major decision to make at the end of the summer, and I didn't even know it. The Viet Nam war was in full bloom. If I stayed in school, I would likely be drafted as soon as I graduated. I made the decision to join the Marine Corps Reserve at the end of the summer. I think some of my friends thought I was crazy, and I'm sure my folks did, but it turned out to be a good decision looking back years later. I signed up at the Fort Worth Marine Reserve Unit, and they swore me in and set the date I was to report for basic training.

Nancy and Jim at a lake near Dallas, Texas

THE MARINES

I HAD ALWAYS been fascinated by the United States Marine Corps. My Uncle Erling was a marine in World War I. I had always heard the training was tough, and they were the best. I hoped I hadn't bitten off more than I could chew, like taking German in summer school.

I went home for a short while, and Nancy came up to meet my parents. I went through Kansas City on my way back to Fort Worth for my official departure. Nancy was in KC to visit her grandmother, we said our goodbyes there, and I was off to Texas. We took a commercial flight to San Diego, California. It was all fun and games on the flight out to California with a lot of laughing and joking and not knowing what awaited us. Our group was met at the San Diego airport in the early evening of an August day. The marine that met us was all business, and our lighthearted mood changed very quickly. We were told to keep our eyes straight ahead and our mouths shut as he marched us out to the sidewalk in front of the airport. Cars drove by with yells coming from inside saying "You'll regret it. Run for your life, sucker." It wasn't too long before a bus arrived to give us a ride to the recruit depot, right next door to the airport. After a short ride we were told to get off the bus as fast as we could. We were taken into a building for processing. The first thing we had to do was get out of our civilian clothes and race into a shower area, again as fast as we could. There were men sliding on the slick concrete floor bare-ass naked when they slipped on the wet floor on their way back to get on military clothes. We were only given a few things the first night and then were sent in a march to our barracks, assigned a bunk, and expected to sleep. I fell asleep after a while, and it seemed I had just closed my eyes and had forgotten where I was, and a mean SOB with a "Smokey the Bear" hat was yelling at us to get our clothes on and get out on "Platoon Street"! We then were sent to the "head" to take care of business. The john—or as we were told to refer to it—the head, was a long trough-like urinal that flowed yellow for about ten minutes straight every morning. We were soon lined up back on Platoon Street in our yellow sweat shirts, green marine trousers, and black boots ready to march to the mess hall.

The first meal didn't taste very good as everyone was too nervous to eat. We were told to take our food as we went through the chow line and sit and eat it without talking. After breakfast we were sent to get haircuts. This wasn't just a little off the side, but rather cut to the skin as close as the clippers could go. You were told if you had a mole on your head, you were to put your finger on it or it would end up on the floor. We all looked alike after the haircuts. We then were given a physical, several shots by way of an air gun, and the rest of our gear. We were marched back to the barracks to put our gear into our own foot locker. The rifle we were checked out was to be hung at the foot of out bed, and we were never to be without our cover, or as we used to call it, our hat.

The first few days were a blur, and it took some time to learn the military jargon. It wasn't long, and we were into a routine, and I actually began to enjoy it. I learned to keep my mouth shut and do as I was told, without question. I got in the best shape I had ever been in, ate three healthy meals a day, and slept eight hours a night. We didn't have candy, pop, or much spare time to get into trouble. I actually became gung ho and seemed to enjoy the training. We spent time learning about Marine Corps history, how to drill, rifle nomenclature, first aid, and much other useful and not-so-useful information. I was a little older than some of the recruits, and after I learned what was expected, I wasn't as uptight.

Mail call came every day, and I really looked forward to it. It was the one link to the outside world and also my link to a romance that had been put on hold. Nancy was very devout at writing me every day, and I really looked forward to getting her letters. One day we were lined up on Platoon Street, and my name was called to come up and retrieve a letter. I ran forward, but when I got there, I was told to open the letter because, when the envelope shook, there was more than a letter inside. I opened it to find a few pieces of gum that Nancy had sent me. The drill instructor told me to put the gum in my mouth, wrappers and all, and chew it while giving him twenty pushups. I started doing the pushups while chewing the gum, but when he looked away, I spit the gum and wrappers in the dirt. The

DI soon came back to me and asked to see the gum. I was told now to find it, put it back in my mouth, dirt and all, while I GAVE HIM TWENTY MORE PUSHUPS. Needless to say, I wrote Nancy a nasty letter telling her not to send any more gum!

The only other time I remember getting into trouble was when my mother sent me some cookies she had baked, but the DI ate those while he watched me do pushups. I was made a squad leader and marched to the front of the third squad where ever we were sent. The drill instructor would yell commands as we worked on our drilling capabilities on a huge drill deck. A command was given just as an airplane was taking off from the airport right next door. The loud noise of the plane would drown out the DI's command, and some or our entire platoon would miss the command. We were then told to halt and assume the front leaning rest position, which meant pushups for the whole platoon. This made us in even better shape and also helped our hearing.

You could tell what stage a platoon was in their training by the way they were dressed. Early recruits were called canaries because they had yellow sweatshirts or t-shirts, and their trousers weren't bloused. The further into the training, the more together the recruits looked. You could also tell the new recruits by their eating habits. The longer I was there, the better I ate, even taking food off the new recruit's plates as they headed for the trash can to throw it away.

Boot camp lasts a certain number of weeks. During war the time may be shortened by a week to pump out more Marines in less time. I recall boot camp as about nine weeks. Many of the recruits I went through with were later sent to Viet Nam to fight in an unpopular war. We had a fair number of reserves in our platoon who didn't have to go overseas. I would have gone had I been activated, but don't regret that I wasn't. If I had been sent, I would have preferred to go while still gung-ho from my training. Somewhere in the middle of our training we had a week of "mess duty." We had the job of setting up and cleaning up for the three meals served to all the recruits and drill instructors every day all week. It didn't take the whole platoon, so there was just about one squad of men assigned to do this at our mess hall. I was in charge of the squad, since I was the squad leader. Each squad member was given a task that they did the whole week. We had line people, garbage people, pan washers, etc. I was a floater that would help out where needed. The guys in our group were really good workers. One day, towards the end of the week, we were told if we finished the noon cleanup by 1500 hours, we would get a two-hour break that afternoon. We worked our butts off to make the deadline. We made it! "Ok recruits, you did such a good job we have a special duty for you. The next two hours you will do a deep clean and wax the floor and still be ready for supper." We worked hard to finish our duties, but felt deceived by our superiors. When the end of our week came, we were told that we were the best "mess hall" group they had ever had. It is amazing what a compliment does to your morale, even for a thankless job like mess duty. Every night after our work was finished, I was to march the group back to our Quonset hut. I can still hear the cadence the drill instructor would bark as we marched. I tried to yell the cadence in the same way and felt I did a fairly good job as we marched back without any supervision. Everyone was in a good mood, being done with our duty and having done it well. One of the men had the "talent" of walking on his hands. I was looking over the marching formation when I saw the last man in formation upside down. He was actually quite good at walking on his hands, but before I could stop him, another drill instructor from another platoon witnessed this unorthodox behavior. We were both reported to our DI and whatever "mess duty" PR had taken place the last week was erased. We both had to do pushups for the whole platoon.

Speaking was not encouraged in recruit training. When a recruit wanted to say anything to the DI, he had to ask permission. "Sir, Private Grabau requests permission to speak to the drill instructor, sir." A bark would come back, "Speak, you slimy maggot." "Sir, the private requests permission to make a head call, sir." Another bark, "Two minutes, you puke," came from the drill instructor. A word that was never to be used was "I." Early in our training, before we learned the correct way to speak, the "I" word would come up quite often. The drill instructor would reply in a loud shout, "Eye. This is an eye," he said, pointing to his eye, "and the private had better get his slimy eyeballs off me." Another no-no word was "you." If the recruit said "you," the drill instructor would yell, "Ewe," "ewe." Do I look like a female sheep?" It didn't take long to realize it was better to just keep your mouth shut and spend most of your time listening.

We were soon ready to go to the rifle range to qualify with our M-14. We took buses to the range at Camp Pendleton where we were trained how to hold our rifles and also shoot them. I had my own rifle at home, so it wasn't totally foreign to me. The practice sessions were called snapping in. We learned how to fire from four positions: standing, kneeling, sitting, and prone. We fired from different distances with the closest being standing and the furthest prone. In the prequalification days, I shot marksman and was close to expert. Then the day of the final arrived. We were all nervous because to not qualify was the worst. They only gave you the one chance in boot camp, and if you didn't do it, you were a "non-qual," and wore no qualification medal on your uniform. I did qualify, but not as high as I had hoped for with only a marksman score. I received a square marksman medal that had the nickname "toilet seat." Later in my reserve unit, I qualified twice as an expert which I was much prouder of, and I got crossed rifles to wear on my uniform. We were all relieved when qualification was over. We were taken on a forced march after qualification. Those that did not qualify had to fill their back packs with rocks for the march.

When we were staying at the rifle range barracks, I got a letter from Nancy just before lights out. I slipped out of my bunk to get closer to an outside light so I could read it. This was a bad idea, and I lost my position of squad leader for a short time. I kept working hard and was later given the position back. We were now getting close to graduation from boot camp. They gave us group tests in drill, academics, and physical fitness, to name a few. The marksmanship was also part of the testing. The platoon that did the best in each of these areas was awarded a banner to be attached to the platoon's standard that was carried on every march. Our platoon #2083 won academics and physical fitness awards, which we proudly carried on our standard. We were also put through a number of inspections on the drill deck by the commanders of the recruit depot. Everyone was dressed in uniform as neat as possible, and rifles were cleaned and re-cleaned.

The recruit that carries the standard is called the guide. I was not given that responsibility during most of boot camp. A Private Bernard had that honor for most of the nine weeks. Just before the end of boot camp, Bernard and I were called in to be interviewed by several officers and our drill instructor. It wasn't long after the interview that my drill instructor, Sgt. Comstock, called me into his office and informed me I had won the Honorman Award and would receive a dress blue uniform given by a marine publication called *Leatherneck Magazine.*

Captain Holland and PFC Grabau in dress blues

I did carry the standard for our graduation ceremony. I felt a little awkward since I hadn't done it that much, but things went well, and we were now officially marines. The top ten percent of the platoon were promoted to Private First Class, so we thought we were hot stuff.

I was able to make a call after graduation to say hi to Nancy. There was a long line by the phone booths, but it was well worth the wait. My excitement was tempered by the news that Nancy's best friend, Carolyn Clemmons, had been killed in a plane crash just a day before my graduation. I felt so bad not being there for her in such a great time of sorrow.

Right after graduation we were sent to Camp Pendleton for combat training and then to a specialized school to learn our specialty. I learned to be a 0800 cannon cocker for 105 howitzers. We ended up at Twenty Nine Palms, California, for the duration of our training. I was really ready to get back to school and finish my formal education. I hope I never finish my total education because we should continue to learn as long as we are alive.

I lived in an apartment that was located just a block from campus my final year of school. A mixture of students and nonstudents lived there. I remember a guy that lived directly above us in the two story complex who worked the night shift and would return home at two or three in the morning. My roommate and I would be sleeping and be awakened by the sound of twenty-pound boots being tossed from one side of the room to the other and hitting the hard wood floor with a thud. Then he would roll a golf ball across the floor for his small dog, with large toe nails, to retrieve. The dog made a sound similar to rain drops on a tin roof. One night my roommate, Ross Brackett, got up at three in the morning, put on his golf clothes and shoes, walked up the stairs with clubs and all, pounded on this guy's door, and asked if he could play through.

Ross had been raised in Fort Worth and knew the streets like the back of his hand. One night we were lying in our beds and were just about asleep when we both heard a car going through the gears on the street near our apartment. Ross said, "I hope the guy knows that the street has a big dip in it just two blocks down." Just then we heard a crash in the distance, and it didn't sound good. We got up, dressed, and walked down to see what happened. The car was a late model Corvette that we had heard. When it hit the dip in the road, it became air borne and flew right into a tree. One passenger was killed and the other hurt badly.

Ross was a great guy to room with, and we had a lot of fun my senior year. I wasn't as active in the fraternity, but did get better grades. I was determined to get my degree and finish school on a good note. I had to finish my language requirement and took Spanish my final summer at TCU. I also managed a swimming association with Nancy after we were married June 1, 1968, in Dallas.

I graduated in August of 1968, in between my two weeks of summer camp. I had to get special permission to come back for graduation from summer camp that was held at Fort Sill, Oklahoma, that year. My parents came down to witness this once-in-a-life-time event, and I think they were very proud, or maybe just amazed.

I graduated with a BA in psychology and a minor in biology. I had, at one time, thought of going to law school and wanted a liberal arts education. Nancy and I packed our things and headed back to God's country, Iowa. I went to work for my dad's construction company in September of 1968. I later took some courses in the Construction Engineering Department at Iowa State University to help me in my new career. Believe it or not, I was asked a few years later to teach a class in the same department, which I did for a semester, as an assistant professor. Dr Tom Jillenger was the head of the department, and they needed some instructors with a little practical experience, and I had about as little as anyone. It was a great experience, and I'm sure I learned more than the students.

JOBS

I RECALL MY first experience in trying to earn some money was when my dad had a job in Ogden that was an elementary school building. He told my sister, Emily, and me that we could earn a quarter a window for the simple task of washing them. Wow! We were going to be rich because this school had a lot of windows. They were small ones that were either stationary or opened out. We were given cleaning supplies consisting of some glass cleaner and rags and taken to the job early one morning to get started. Our thoughts were not on the task so much as they were on how we would spend the money. It was only about a half hour into our money machine job that we realized this was going to be a lot of work. I think our dad realized this was more of a lesson than an opportunity to exploit child labor. I don't recall how long we lasted, but suffice to say, we didn't finish the job, and very little money exchanged hands.

I did the typical jobs around the house to earn my allowance. I emptied the garbage, learned to mow the yard, and cleaned out the garage. I didn't realize it at the time, but I was developing a work ethic that would last a life time. Some of the jobs were not done without my parents nagging at me to do them, but I did learn that it was necessary to do my part. I watched my dad and mother both work hard for whatever they had, and it may have happened subconsciously, but I slowly gained the appreciation of hard work.

We didn't have live stock on the acreage I grew up on, but the Gustafsons did. They lived just a quarter of a mile to our south and had three boys, Doug, Steve, and Mark. They had an acreage too, but with a few cows and hogs as well as some chickens. They had to complete their chores in order to be allowed to play, and if I helped, we would have more play time. I became the fourth Gustafson boy. We did everything from sloping hogs to hand picking corn. When I got a little older, I was invited to help walk beans with them on farms that Doug, who was two years older than I, would line up. This was, of course, before miracle chemicals such as Round-up, and it was necessary to pull or cut the weeds out of the beans. We would walk four abreast through the bean rows with each of us responsible for three or so rows on each side of us. Once in a while Mark, the youngest of the Gustafson brothers, would miss a weed, and I would tell him. Doug was very quick to tell me he would take care of Mark, and I should watch my own rows, which I then did. We walked fields for the Stott's, the Anderson's, and many others. We would start early in the morning and work until about noon. This was fine with me because I then could go to the pool in the afternoon. I was about fourteen at the time, and my summer recreation consisted of playing baseball and hanging out at the pool.

I don't recall how old I was when I got a paper route for the afternoon paper of the *Des Moines Register* and *Tribune*. The afternoon version was called the *Tribune*. My route was on the north side of Boone, which was good since I lived on the northeast corner of town, a quarter mile out of the city limits. The first day I was to deliver my papers, it was raining cats and dogs. I had always lived in the country and didn't know much about the way homes were numbered in town. I had several deliveries to numbers that ended in ½. I couldn't figure out where these homes would be. It didn't help that it was pouring down rain, and my papers were getting wet. I felt total frustration and was ready to quit when a boy by the name of Mark Rasmus helped me finish my route and told me the half numbers were for apartments, and even numbers were on one side of the street, and odd numbers on the other. I really appreciated this help, and we became friends and still are today. I still have a punch bowl he gave us for our wedding over forty years ago.

Boone's downtown retail area was healthy when I was a teenager. I really wanted to get a part time job at one of the stores to make money of my own and also gain experience. I applied at a number of retail stores and finally was hired to work at the Coast to Coast hardware store. The first thing I learned to do was put bikes, wagons, and other toys together in the basement of the store. I did get better at reading step-by-step directions of how each of the items was assembled. There were times when the store got busy that I got to see the light of day and was asked to wait on customers on the main floor. I did not have any experience at this and would sometimes become so nervous that I would make a mistake. This job was teaching me some people skills as well as how to make change and that the customer was always right. I worked at this job for about a year, but wanted to become a carry-out for Lawson's Grocery Store. I was still fifteen, and Chet Lawson, the owner, said I needed to be sixteen before he would hire me. I was persistent and kept asking him, and he finally gave in. My mother shopped there a lot because we had helped remodel the store and some of the payment was in groceries. This was most likely why I was given the job. Having a job was a rite of passage in a small town and gave you some independence as well as a certain status. I was very pleased to be a carry out and stock boy at Lawson's, the store with the magic door. Lawson's was the first store in Boone to have an automatic self-opening door, and it became their signature line.

My boss, Chet, and his wife, Gladys, were very hard workers and had the same expectations of their employees. My starting wage was fifty cents per hour, and in the summer I would work as many as forty-five to fifty hours per week. The job was fairly simple and consisted of helping people out with their groceries and stocking the shelves between carry out service. We would also unload trucks and do whatever we were told. The time went quickly, and with a lot of contact with customers, I learned some people skills. "Would you like your things in a box or a sack?" was the question asked over and over throughout the day. This was before the flimsy plastic sacks they have now. Boxes from supplies that had been shipped to the store were brought to the "box bin" and used to pack the purchased products in to take home. This really worked well as it got rid of the boxes and provided a great means to carry the groceries. Sometimes the customers wanted small boxes so they wouldn't be too heavy, and some preferred sacks. A large order consisted of three or four sacks and would cost about twenty dollars. When you go to the store now, you don't need a carry out for twenty dollars worth of groceries any more. We seldom used a cart to carry out the bags or boxes and took great pride in being loaded with as much as we could carry. Another carry out, Henry Schmidt, and I would have a contest to see who could carry the most. We also were taught a certain way to pack the groceries with a good foundation, sturdy items to the bottom and soft items at the top, and *don't break the eggs*!

The Lawson's were very frugal, and they wasted very little. They would buy bulk potatoes in one hundred-pound bags. We would then dump these out on the floor in the back room and fill ten pound bags to sell. There were always some rotten ones in the large bag. We would take these and slice off the rotten part, and Gladys would take them home and bring back home made potato salad. When some bananas had black spots, she would take them home and return with homemade banana nut bread to sell in the store. They even ordered bulk vinegar in large oak barrels that we would strain, and then pump into gallon glass jugs to sell during the pickle season. There would be fewer hungry people if we all conserved as well as the Lawsons did. Working for Chet and Gladys was the start to a great foundation of learning the meaning of a hard day's work.

The summer after I graduated from high school, I went to work for my dad as summer help. The first job I worked on was the Boone National Guard Armory that the company built in 1963. I recall going home for lunch at noon and returning an hour later. The superintendent asked if I had fish for lunch. I said "No, why did you ask me that?" He said, "We only take a half hour for lunch, and I thought you needed the extra time to get the bones out of your teeth." He laughed. I was embarrassed because at the grocery store we were given a full hour. I brought my lunch after that and was never late again. I worked all summer for R. H. Grabau Construction and started my freshman year at the Boone Junior College in the fall. I would sometimes work on the weekends for the company if I was needed.

I worked summers mostly as a laborer, but my dad also thought it would be good for me to learn a trade. Dad had learned to be an accomplished brick mason, and he thought that it would be good for me to learn the trade at least in part during the summer. I became a "cub" mason at the county home in Fort Dodge. I would ride to the job every day with LaVern Condon, my Dad's most experienced superintendent. The areas that I worked were usually in a location that wouldn't show, so it didn't have to be perfect, and it wasn't. I never became proficient at the trade but was better by the end of the summer than at the beginning.

My last two summers at TCU were spent in summer school, the Marines, and then summer school and managing a swim association. In order to graduate I had to pick up my final six hours of a language requirement in summer school. Nancy and I were married in June, and with only three hours to take each semester of summer school, I thought I had better get a job. I found out that the Western Hills Swimming Association was looking for a manager, so I applied. I had my life saving as well as a water safety instructor certification. I had been on the TCU swim team during its beginning period. I went to the interview, and low and behold, they hired me.

The pool was not very big, but was long enough for a junior swim team, which I coached in the early morning. After swim team, we taught swim lessons until noon for the younger age groups. Nancy helped with the younger children, and I also had an assistant manager and a couple of life guards. The afternoon was spent lifeguarding and selling concessions. The pool was open until early evening, and members could also schedule parties until later for a fee. The work wasn't hard, but the days were long. I never thought I would get sick of being in the sun, but by the end of summer, I had blond hair and was as dark as I could tan. Remember, this was before we worried about skin cancer and sun screen was called zinc oxide and was only used on your nose.

I had a lot of fun coaching the age group team with ages from eight to fifteen. One little boy said to me during time trials that the water was way too hard or he would swim faster. This was my first attempt at coaching, and I had a lot to learn. I bought a book and also drew from other swim coaches I had in earlier years. It was rewarding to see the progress all the team members made over the summer.

We competed in several meets during the summer, and they won some individual trophies and medals. One of the meets was held in a fifty-meter Olympic pool in Fort Worth. The little kids really freaked out when they saw how long fifty meters is in one stretch.

The end of the summer came quickly, and Nancy and I thought it would be fun to host a party with some of our friends from Fort Worth, Dallas, and even Oklahoma being invited. It was to have a Hawaiian theme, with bright shirts, dresses, fruit, and some great punch. We would go to the pool first and then come back to eat, or was it the other way around? A pledge brother, and later a fraternity brother of mine by the name of Ken Field, was to drive down from Oklahoma City for the party and stay with us. Ken arrived in the middle of the afternoon while Nancy was out getting groceries for the party. He had parked, and let himself in to get ready. I was working at the pool and would be home later. Nancy arrived back with the groceries, and with a bag in each arm, came back into the small house we were renting. She noticed the bathroom door slightly open and became suspicious that it might be a boogeyman. The smart thing to do would have been to leave quickly, and quietly, and seek some help, but that is not what she did. Instead she went to the bathroom door with arms still full with the groceries and gave it a karate kick, making the door fly open. Behind the door sat my friend Ken having his daily constitution. Without a word said, Nancy quickly went to the kitchen, and Ken tried to finish what he had started. This may explain why it took Ken until his forties to get married.

The party came off well, and we had a great time. Many years later I had the opportunity to tell this story at Ken's rehearsal dinner, much to Ken's chagrin. I graduated in August of 1968 from TCU, and we were ready to head north to Iowa. I have one more story to tell about our little home we were leaving in Fort Worth. I think it was originally built as a maid's quarters behind a rather large, pretentious home. The lady we rented from had a son that was a little on the wild side. He used to steal beer from the Budweiser delivery man while he was inside a neighborhood store and ride off with it on his bicycle. Towards the end of the summer, they decided to sell the two homes. They were also selling the furniture out of our rental property. Every night when we came home from the pool, we would discover another piece of our rented furnishings missing: first a desk, then a lamp, a rug, and finally our bed. I contacted a fraternity brother who was an attorney and asked him what to do? He wrote a letter telling them that the furniture was part of the lease agreement, and the buyer then furnished our apartment for the balance of our stay. We took a picture of us sitting on the bare floor with candles and nothing else in the apartment before it was refurnished.

We were ready to pack up our meager belongings to drive to Iowa, but we had one last task, sell Nancy's Corvair. We had waited until the last minute to "unload" her white two-door Corvair so Nancy wouldn't have to drive it to Iowa. The car had the unique feature of running the exhaust through the heater, which was not only left a bad smell in the car but also could kill you. We hadn't thought far enough ahead to put an ad in the classifieds, so we would go from dealer to dealer to see who would be the lucky buyer. Had we kept it, the car now would be a collector's dream, but back then it was an albatross. We would shut off the engine and coast into these dealerships so the car would sound quiet. We finally found a dealer that gave us only about two or three hundred dollars for it.

The drive to Iowa and, more specifically, Boone, takes about twelve hours. We had rented a U-Haul, so it may have been a little longer. We arrived safely to our home located at 1409 Aldrich. My dad had taken the liberty to purchase a house that was being displaced by a restaurant on Story Street. He hired a company to move the house to a lot he had purchased on Aldrich. A new block basement was built, and the house was set on the basement. He had Grabau Construction build a new fire place and install new kitchen cupboards. We assumed the home loan at what I am sure was less than he had invested. The payments were ninety dollars a month for what to us was a brand new house. The house had two small bedrooms, a living room, dining room, TV room, and full unfinished basement. Needless to say we were very excited and thankful to my dad. A few years down the line, we added a third bedroom and a detached garage.

The first job I worked on for Grabau Construction was Hawkeye Savings and Loan, which was building a new bank and office where the old post office had been. It was a shame the old stone building was torn down because it was a very stately building of Indiana limestone and had historical significance. I worked outside that first winter back in Iowa learning the field under LaVern Condon. Paul

Miller was also on the job, and those two taught me a lot. We spent most of the winter forming EFCO walls that were then poured full of concrete and later stripped to start the process all over again. The concrete had to be kept from freezing so after a pour, we would cover the wall and heat the area with salamander heaters and propane gas. The cylinders were only ninety pounds and often had to be changed in the middle of the night. The whole process was good experience for me and helped me appreciate the field workers.

I kept the time sheets and the labor breakdown sheets for the project, and this helped me understand the flow of costs to provide data for bidding future projects. The first project I was given responsibility for running—using the term lightly—was the Slater, Iowa, school. Paul Miller was sent with me to "hold my hand," and that was a good idea because I was still pretty green. This was the first time I met Bill Dryer of Rudi, Lee, and Dryer Architects of Ames. Bill was the architect, and we worked together several times over our careers.

It took me a while, but I soon learned that in the construction industry, you cross paths with people in the business many times over in your lifetime. It is just good business to treat people well because you are going to work with them again someday. Don't burn bridges.

The Slater school was not a very big project, but it was large enough to teach me some of the basics. When you are in charge, the whole game is changed. You have to be able to make decisions and live with them. We finished the project and went through the punch list process. Punch lists are not for the "thin skinned." They can be tough on your ego when something you did does not meet the architect's standard of quality. You then have to fix items so they pass inspection, so to speak. This is done until everything passes, and you finally get the last payment on the project.

I took some construction courses at Iowa State University to better educate me for my career. One of my instructors who taught cost estimating was Norm Riis. I enjoyed his class and learned many things. We later became good friends with both Norm and Rita Riis through our association with the Master Builders of Iowa. These are the relationships that have meant the most to me over the forty years that I have been in the construction industry. I was later asked to teach a course in the Construction Engineering Department by Tom Jillenger, the first Professor-in-charge. This was a very rewarding experience, and I'm sure I learned more than my students.

The first job on which I did the takeoff and estimating was Saint Cecilia Catholic church in Ames. I was very green at this as well, and I think I left something out of my bid. I was, of course, very nervous and asked my dad if I could run the job, too, in hopes of keeping the overhead down. He let me do that, and I think we came out ok on the job. One of the men that worked for us during this job was Bruce Beerman, a former Iowa State football player from New Jersey. This was now the seventies, and Bruce had dropped out of school, stopped playing football, and became somewhat of a "flower child." We had some interesting conversations but a major difference in life styles. Bruce was a good worker and had a great sense of humor. He worked his way up to become a superintendent and even his philosophy became much more conservative. He went back to school, got his degree, and even after he left our company, we have remained friends.

Bruce told me of a trick he would do at parties called the wizard. He would tell people at a party that he knew a wizard that could tell what card someone had chosen out of a deck of cards from long distance. He would then place a call to the wizard, which now had become me, to identify the card. I would usually be asleep, and it would be one o'clock in the morning. I would try to wake myself up when Bruce would say to me over the phone, "Is the wizard there?" This was my cue to go through the suits of the cards, such as hearts, diamonds, spades, and clubs. When I got to the one the person at the party had chosen, Bruce would say, "Yes, the wizard." This was my cue that I had said the right suit. The next thing I was to do was go through the numbers starting with the ace and up to whatever card had been chosen. When I said the right card, Bruce would say over the phone, "Yes, the wizard," and I knew I had the right card and suit. He would then hand the phone to the party guest for them to hear me say in a low mysterious voice the card they had chosen, "The ace of clubs," and I would quickly hang up. No one would guess that someone was on "call" every Saturday night to be an accomplice in such a charade.

Roger Temple worked for the company as a book keeper first and then an estimator. I learned many things from Roger as well. He was very meticulous and good at what he did. The bid sheets we used were all written out in long hand on special lined paper we bought from The Boone Blank & Book Company. We would underline the headings such as Demolition, Carpentry, etc., for the entire scope of the job. This was before computers, digitizers, fax machines, and even digital calculators. The process of taking off a job with a scale rule and colored pencil took a long time. On some of the larger jobs we would work together with each of us responsible for a portion of the print. This process could take up to two or three weeks. We would then have to plug unit costs in for each item and extend the calculations with a mechanical calculator. The calculator was about twelve inches square and weighed thirty or more pounds. It made a sound like a trashing machine when it did the calculations. A digital calculator in the nineties that cost less than ten dollars could do the same calculations. The last mechanical calculator I used cost $750. Looking back, it's hard to believe I have seen so many technological changes in my life time.

Mary Youngblood was hired right out of high school as a secretary. She later became office manager and then treasurer and finally controller for the company. I can recall a major decision as to whether we needed a fax machine when they first came out. Before there were fax machines, Mary would have to write out long hand phone quotes that could be several pages long. She had to read the quote back to them to make sure it was correct. You would think that the quotes would come in over several days before the letting, but they almost all come in during the final two hours and many in the last half hour. Everyone should have the opportunity of putting a bid together at least once in their life. It is a combination of an adrenalin rush and sheer panic as your brain tries to think of so many things at one time, and thousands of dollars are at stake. Technology has helped to ease the feeling of "too much to do in too little time," but there are still times when you have to make big decisions in a very short time. We used to have the bid together and ready for the final number with an add and deduct sheet to tally when lower bids from suppliers and subcontractors would come in. This worked better than trying to erase numbers on the estimate and re-total every time there was a change. You have to remember we didn't have a computer to automatically re-total everything when a number was changed.

Another challenge to bidding a project is the alternates that are included with the bid package. I can remember jobs that had as many as ten alternates that had to be figured in the bidding process. This is usually caused by a weak architect that doesn't know how to tell the owner that one or two alternates is plenty, and they don't need to put the contractors through so many hoops to find out if they can afford five hundred more square feet on their building.

I really enjoyed my time out in the field running a job or helping complete a task. I learned to operate a crane we had that was a Koering 205 cable operation. It would never pass today's safety standards, and we finally got rid of it. I helped LaVern Condon pour concrete at the Citizens National Bank in Boone by operating the crane. He had taught me how to operate the crane, and you had to be very cautious with the controls with each operation. There were high voltage power lines that ran over the construction area that made the job more complicated. Electricity can arc from these lines to the steel crane boom, and this is not a good thing. I did like the fact that I could do something constructive out in the field, and to quote a line from the movie, "Six Days and Seven Nights," that Harrison Ford said, "I'm not without skills." I was able to do a lot of different construction activities from running equipment such as John Deere crawlers and skid loaders to pouring concrete and finishing it. I didn't do any of them long enough to become an expert, but I at least gained an appreciation of the jobs the field personal do. Looking back at my career in the construction industry, one thing comes clear more than any other, and that is the relationships that were developed with other people in the industry. Some of these were with designers, others with employees, and others with owners. It is difficult to be in the construction industry without some friction developing with the people you work with, be it an architect, a subcontractor, or an employee. I'm sure when I was younger, I over reacted to many of these conflicts. I became a little mellower as I matured and got older. You don't want to burn too many bridges because you will be working with these same people sometime in the future. The friendships that have developed greatly outweigh the conflicts over my career. I have found lifelong friends in this business from some of my competitors, employees, suppliers, and designers.

The Master Builders of Iowa is a chapter of the National Association of General Contractors. R. H. Grabau Construction became a member of this organization in 1949 and has been a member ever since. I first attended a MBI function when I was just seven years old at the summer picnic held at Lake Okoboji. It became an event I looked forward to all year long. I was there, of course, just for the fun, but even then I made friends that lasted through my lifetime. When I became older and part of the business, I still looked forward to the meetings and summer activities. There was some learning mixed with fun and activities that created a great place to meet and make friends. We would pack up the family every year and head to this "picnic meeting" for a long weekend. They would have golf and tennis tournaments, which were also great opportunities to meet and get to know people.

I first became active in the MBI after college, and I started my career with Grabau Construction. I would go to the meetings rather than just the fun activities I had when I was younger. I was there to learn as well as meet people from other firms and see how they ran their firms.

A unique thing about the MBI is the vast range of companies that are members. Companies range from some of the largest in the country to the smallest. I never felt that my voice was any less because our firm wasn't the largest company in the organization. I tend to speak my piece at meetings and, because of this, would soon find myself in some capacity of leadership. I recall the first committee I served on was the summer meeting planning committee. Imagine that! It was this group's duty to plan the food and activities for the long weekend. Many of the activities were set by "tradition," so our biggest decision was the food that would be served. I loved the way the owners of Vacation Village would describe the different meals they could prepare and how delicious they would be. One thing the contractors' group was good at was eating. We had at least four meals a day, not to mention a cocktail party with hors d'oeuvres. We had breakfast, lunch, and dinner, and then have a brat roast late in the evening to sleep on.

I became chairperson of the summer meeting after a few years of serving on the committee. Just before we left to drive up to the summer meeting, we were at a church function, and a group did a really funny skit with costumes of a large top hat put over a man's shoulders, and a face painted on the man's bare chest, with large eyes and lips painted at the navel. Below the lips is a suit with arms and white gloves to make it look like a short man with a big head. We thought it was so funny that we asked if we could borrow the costumes to take to the lake. They said that would be fine, so we thought this would be added entertainment. We had no idea who we would get to wear the outfits once we got to Okoboji. A contractor by the name of Hugo Gerhels was one of our choices, and he was a good sport and agreed to do it. I don't remember who we got to be in the second outfit, but we found someone. The part that made it really funny was once dressed, they were to whistle with their stomachs going in and out to make it look like their navel "lips" were blowing air. While this was going on, a record with a whistling song that they kept beat with was played in the background. I think we had the "Bridge Over River Qui" done in a whistle as their music.

The crowd that would gather for the evening of fun and fellowship just went crazy, they were laughing so loud. The smaller children thought these were special little people, and the adults knew what they were looking at, and everyone thought it was hilarious. It went over so well, we found two other guinea pigs to do it the second night. I wish I had taken some pictures to remember the fun we had those nights. The MBI was, and still is, a great organization that I enjoyed as a kid, and later as an adult. The friendships and the relationships have lasted the test of time.

When tennis was just as popular as golf, the committee put together a tennis tournament for those willing to participate at the summer meeting. Jim Seaman, a staff member of the MBI, would put groups together using bridge tabs to organize a system where everyone would play each other. There were two courts, so eight people could play at one time. It was a modification of mixed doubles with scores kept for each person's number of games won. There would normally be two separate groups, and the eight with the highest scores would play a second round to determine winners in both a men's and women's totals. When we were finished playing, John and Julie Holtze would have a whole case of champagne for the group to quench their thirst. On a hot day it is not a good idea to quench your thirst with champagne because your speech soon becomes distorted. One year a storm came through, and we all ended up in a basement of the caretaker's house, until it passed. We always had a lot of fun, and for the most part I behaved, even though I liked to win.

I continued to serve on committees and eventually was elected to the board. My dad had served a term on the board years ago, and it is a great experience. When I served, it was a three-year term, unless you became president, and then it was four years because you stayed on one additional year as an ex-official member. The succession to president came by being elected by the board to vice president, and the following year you were president. David Holtze was the president when I became VP. You don't realize it at the time, but you learn so many things from the leaders that are in front of you. Dave was a down to business guy and taught me many things I used throughout my career.

Another neat thing about the MBI was the trips we took. About every four years the MBI would have a meeting outside the country. The first trip like this that Nancy and I went on was to Acapulco, Mexico. I remembered my folks going on some of these and had always thought it would be fun. We had been to Acapulco twice before and had developed a love affair with Mexico. These trips weren't too long because they tried to keep the cost down and would have a seminar during the trip to keep the IRS happy. It was a time when you got to know people better and could let your "hair down," so to speak. We went on several of these trips over the years to several tropical places including Jamaica and Aruba.

The year I became Vice President of the MBI, they sent me to Boston, Washington DC, and Hawaii. I always have a knack for being in the right place at the right time. I became President of the MBI in 1987. It was an interesting year when some really good things happened, but also some challenging things. The MBI had started its own workers' compensation insurance program. We thought we had done everything right, but sometimes even that isn't enough. The year had some bad experiences, and our reinsurer went belly up as well. We had to close out of this program and made it out by the skin of our teeth. That same year we were challenged by the State Attorney General and had to change our support agreement to a different fee structure. Sometimes adversity gives birth to ingenuity, and in this case our plan room and job reporting service more than picked up the slack. Some of these things occured over two or three years, and I may not have the exact times correct. We still had a great year and were awarded The Associated General Contractors Chapter of the Year Award at the convention held in New Orleans in early 1988. Jim Ryan, the Executive Secretary, Mike Carlstrom, and I were sent to the convention to receive the award. It was a neat honor for the MBI, and Jim Ryan and the membership deserve most of the credit. The staff does all the work behind the scenes and then lets the leadership have the credit.

In August of 1987 my dad died at the age of eighty on the 24th of the month. He had gotten late onset diabetes when he was seventy-five, and it finally wore his heart out. What a great father and mentor he was to me, and I appreciate it more the older I become. He gave me a job and an opportunity to do something I enjoyed my whole working life. He never really retired in any official way and would still come to the office to check on what was going on. I remember his big smile the most, and he had a way of always making you feel better in good times or bad. My mother lived another thirteen years and died in the year 2000 at the age of ninety-three. Both of my parents were very generous to me with both love and financial support and I am very grateful.

Grabau Construction has had some very dedicated employees, and I can't mention them all, but some of the early ones include LaVern Condon, Johnny and Lyle Paris, Paul Lilly, Paul Miller, Roger Temple, Bruce Beerman, Rocky Grillo, and current ones include Mary Youngblood, Eric Hammer, Kevin Porter, Rob Eckard, and Troy Nordholm. Larry Welder was also a good superintendent, and we have had a lot of loyal, hard working employees over the years. I don't want to diminish their importance by not mentioning their names. Maybe we should have become bigger over these last sixty-some years, but we put a lot of kids through school and tried to maintain balance in our lives so it isn't just about work but about life. I love my job and enjoy work, but as I get older, I could use less risk in my life financially.

I am sixty three as I write this, and I was given a nice honor this February by the Master Builders of Iowa. In 1989 the MBI established a recognition award to someone they feel exemplifies the tenants of the organization, which are skill, integrity, and responsibility. My office staff, with the collaboration of Story Construction of Ames, nominated me for the award. This year they announced the award in advance and had a reception rather than a dinner for the award night. They had a big picture of me as people came in, and it was a little embarrassing. I was honored to be selected, and I mentioned in my acceptance that I felt it is a company award as they enabled me to become involved in the things I did. I invited my sister and Alan, my neighbors Pete and Mary Bilden, Rick and Barb Wulkow, and Gary and Kathy Nystrom. The company was represented by Mary Youngblood and Dick, Eric Hammer and Julie, and Kevin Porter and Brenda. I had to ask some people to do a brief video on why they thought I deserved the award. Mary Youngblood, Kirke Quinn, Rick Wulkow, Gary Nystrom and Bob Maddox did the montage of video for the ceremony. Most of it was serious, but it also had some comic relief with some funny stories.

General Ron Dardis, the Adjutant General for the Iowa National Guard, gave a keynote address before my award. He did a good job, but it got rather heavy when he spoke of Iowans losing their lives and limbs for their country. After he spoke, I was concerned that my award seemed rather trite compared to the sacrifices these Guard soldiers had made. When I was introduced, I tried to think of a way to smooth out the transition from his speech to my award. I did mention that my award seemed trite and that I try to thank military men and women for their service when I see them in the airport or anywhere, and that we should all try to do this. I then introduced my beautiful wife, Nancy, telling of her father who was a Naval Aviator in WWII and made the ultimate sacrifice in the Pacific. He was awarded The Silver Star for bravery in Africa and after leave was sent to the Pacific and never came back, but he gave me his daughter, Nancy, of whom he would have been very proud. I said Nancy was the best thing that ever happened to me, and that is the truth. I introduced the rest of my guests and spoke briefly about the rich history of the MBI and the importance of involvement. I ended by saying that I don't cast as long a shadow as the others on the list of winners, but am humbled and honored to be included on it, thank you. It was a very memorable evening, and I hope everyone had a good time.

Mary Youngblood, Eric Hammer, and Kevin Porter have entered into an agreement with me to buy the company over ten years starting with my retirement the end of 2010. There are times I wish I were already retired and times I would like to die with my boots on, but I thought it was only fair to set a date for Mary, Eric, and Kevin so they can make plans, and I can go to another chapter of my life, with the Lord willing. They also gave me a "picture scrap book," that is very high quality, with memories from many of my forty years in the construction industry. I can't say enough about what a great privilege it has been to work with these three and many other fine people in the industry.

Nancy

NANCY

I WAS A junior in college, and at that time airlines had discount tickets for different classes to fly. There were military half price fares, student half fares, and semi-free fares for dependents of airline employees. I was going home for Easter and was on a student stand-by, as were most discounted ticket holders. It was a cheaper way to fly, but at holidays sometimes difficult to get on a flight. I mentioned earlier that I met Nancy while we were waiting for a flight home for the holiday. The airport that most flights went out of back then was Love Field, and it was not too far from her home in the Northwood Hills area of Dallas. We both got on the next flight to Kansas City.

After the Easter holiday, I returned to finish my junior year. I was in my room, no doubt studying, when the phone rang, and it was the same Nancy Higley calling. She asked if I would like to go with her to the Pi Phi Formal in a couple weeks. I said sure, and that was the start of what was to become a lifelong love affair. I almost blew the romance before it started. I didn't call her until the night before the dance. It would have been nice if I had taken her out for a Coke or some sort of contact just to be polite. I had some frat brothers that were dating Pi Phi's, so we all went together. We had a great time in spite of several of us guys doing the "gator" on the floor in our good clothes with some even splitting out their trousers. Nancy and I started dating and had some great times doing things like going to the Fort Worth Zoo and seeing Jim, the black bear.

Nancy lived in Dallas, but had grown up in Kansas City and was there until her senior year when her family moved to Dallas. Her step-father was a Braniff pilot, and they moved their base to Texas. It was the policy then that you had to live in the same city where your airline that you flew for had its base. Nancy went to Richardson High School her senior year. Even though she was only there for one year, she was chosen to be Miss Richardson Princess. She chose to go to TCU for her college education in Fort Worth, Texas: a good thing for me since that's where I ended up in 1965.

I went to summer school that summer, the summer I took German, if you recall from my "schools" chapter. A pledge brother of mine, Benny Vinzant, had the use of his father's boat, and we would go water skiing every chance we would get. I had been able to ski on two skis for some time but not until another pledge brother, Mike Bradford, worked with me did I learn to ski slalom. The boat we skied behind was an outboard with a sixty-five horse engine, as I recall. To get two skiers up on one ski each would require a special system. Both skiers would drag one leg and stay down on their ski until the boat got enough speed for them to stay up and then slip their back foot into the ski. It would take about half the distance of the length of a long lake to get the two up. We would then cut back and forth trying to be hot dogs to impress the girls. Nancy was a good skier from times she spent up at Lake Geneva in earlier summers. We would ski all day long, and when we ran out of light, or gas, the boat would usually have some mechanical problem, and we would have to be towed back to shore; pulling that much weight out of the water with a small older motor can't be good for it. Benny's dad later traded the old boat for an inboard outboard that was much more dependable.

I think one of the things I liked about Nancy from the beginning was that she was so natural. She didn't worry that her hair was perfect all the time, and she was just naturally beautiful even after getting out of the "not so clean, man-made lakes" we skied on near Dallas. We both loved the water and all the fun associated with it. I remember Nancy telling me how the fraternity brother that she dated before me got so upset when she had been caught in the rain and her hair wasn't just perfect when she met him for a date. He had said that embarrassed him and would affect how others thought of him. Wow, that made me embarrassed that he was my frat brother! The feature that I still think is one of Nancy's most beautiful is her eyes. They are round in shape and an unusual aqua green in color. I realize beauty is subjective, but the longer you know Nancy, the more beautiful she becomes. She is willing to do fun things and doesn't worry if she is being a little crazy, and she is still that way today.

I mentioned that I joined the Marine Corps Reserve and was out of school for six months. I think this turned out to be a good decision looking back. I came home for leave just before Christmas, and Nancy came to Boone to have an early celebration with my family. They had met her before, but celebrating an early Christmas together was really special. I had to fly back on Christmas Eve, and I recall the pilot flying over the Country Club Plaza to show the passengers the beautiful lights. I was fortunate to get home at all as many soldiers in Viet Nam did not get home, and some didn't make it home alive.

It wasn't too long before Nancy and I were together again. My hair had grown out some since the first time Nancy saw me with my military burr on leave. I went to a fraternity party with her soon after I got back and had no tolerance for alcohol. I wasn't a big drinker, but I must have wanted to celebrate being a civilian again. I drove Nancy home with my head out the window to stay awake and try to get sober again. I think she really wondered if I was the right guy that night. I was pleased again that she didn't dump me. She was staying with a friend at some apartment, and when we found the area, I would leave her in the car and try to find the apartment she was to spend the night. I finally located it, and I was much better behaved after that night.

We continued to date while I worked to finish school. I had saved some money to buy Nancy an engagement ring from George Eckstein at Eckstein's Diamonds. I wasn't very creative about the way I asked Nancy to marry me. I gave her the ring, in the dorm parking lot, at TCU. We had talked about getting married, so it wasn't a big surprise. I had paid about six hundred dollars for the ring, and it was about a .6 carat solitaire. She accepted, so far, so good. I would finish my school, and we would get married in June of 1968. The school year went quickly with all the plans we were making. I selected a date that wouldn't be too hard to remember for future anniversaries, June 1.

We were married on Memorial Day Weekend and didn't have a large turnout. We had the rehearsal dinner on Friday night at a nice hotel downtown Dallas for a small group of family and friends. The restaurant was in the Southland Life building, one of the taller buildings in Dallas at the time. Nancy's Episcopal Church was under construction, so we were married at the Church of The Incarnation in Dallas. A lot of my parents' guests were from Iowa, and our younger friends had gone home for the summer, so although the wedding was very nice, it could have been in a smaller church. Back when we got married, very few weddings had a dinner and dance like most do now. The receptions were held in the church basement or social hall, and guests were served punch, nuts, and cake, and were sent on their way.

Right after the wedding, we left from Love Field in Dallas to fly to Acapulco, Mexico, for our honeymoon. Our parents went out to dinner together at the Zider-Zee Seafood Restaurant. Nancy had been given her last free airline ticket to use on our honeymoon, but almost got bumped in San Antonio on the way to Acapulco. We told the flight attendants that we were on our honeymoon, and they were able to keep us on the flight. When we arrived in Acapulco at our hotel called The Posada Del Sol, it was late in the evening, and we were asked if we were beginners or old timers. Nancy said, "I'm a beginner but I'm not sure about him," pointing at me. It was now June 2, and we had the place to ourselves.

We had been to Acapulco a year before our honeymoon with Nancy's family, so we knew a little bit about the area. We weren't far from the El Presidente, and we would walk down to the large hotel for breakfast. We were waiting for our order when two cooks came running out of the kitchen yelling something in Spanish. We could see smoke coming from behind them and made a good guess that the kitchen was on fire. We headed for the door as did the others having breakfast at the restaurant. We had a great time, and besides the usual honeymoon activities, swimming and sunning, we spent a great deal of time looking for the perfect chess set. For whatever reason, I wanted an onyx chess set to take back to our little apartment. We finally found one and bargained for what we felt was a good price. We started a long tradition of taking something back on the plane that is too heavy, breakable, or large to buy this far from home.

John Kennedy had been killed when I was a freshman at the Boone Junior College. We were walking on the beach one morning in Acapulco when we heard that Robert Kennedy had met the same fate. What a crazy world we live in.

After a week of sun and fun, we returned to Fort Worth for me to finish six hours of Spanish in summer school. I managed the Western Hills Swim Association with the help of Nancy, and went to class at night to graduate in August. We had a fun summer and a busy one with swim team, lessons, and open swim until late in the evening.

Summer went quickly, and we were soon headed for our new home in Iowa. Nancy was a really good sport in coming to live in Iowa and not complaining. She makes friends so easily that where ever she had landed, people were going to like her. The Erbe girls said the first time they saw her, they thought she was a movie star. They told me this year's later as they recalled when we first came back to Boone in 1968.

My dad had purchased a home that was to be demolished, if no one moved it, to make room for a new restaurant. He hired a moving company to move it to a lot he had purchased at 1409 Aldrich. A basement had been dug and block walls laid to form a foundation for the house to be set on. We assumed the loan for the house, at what I am sure was less than full value. I think the entire loan was twelve thousand dollars and our payments, ninety dollars per month. It was a cute home, and we had a lot of fun fixing it up. We would shop for carpet, and Nancy would refinish used furniture by "antiquing" it. We went to lots of auctions to buy other pieces for the home. It all sounds very domestic, but it was a great time in our lives.

Nancy would substitute teach when we first came to Boone, and she then took over a second grade class at the same Franklin school I had attended earlier. We both became active in the local Jaycee chapter to meet young couples as well as contribute to the community. I can recall going to the Jaycee awards banquet and seeing Gary Grosnickle and Lloyd Courter recognized for their efforts in the community. This made a big impression on me and made me want to try to make a difference in our community.

Our first years of marriage went by quickly, and it wasn't long before we were blessed with a baby girl we named Alison; she was ten pounds, seven ounces, and Nancy had some complications after the delivery. Alan Munson, my brother-in-law, was an OBGYN doing his residency in Iowa City. He gave me some good advice, and Nancy ended up in Iowa City for some special care and recovered one hundred percent.

Our not-so-little girl came home, and so did her mother after a short stay in Iowa City. Nancy's grandmother, who had vouched for me when we first met, came up to help with the baby until Nancy was stronger. I can still remember the first night we were on our own and her grandmother had gone back to Kansas City. We knew very little of child care, and this was extreme on-the-job training. I think we both felt sick with the first diaper we changed, but it wasn't too long before we could change and feed her while we were still half asleep.

Twenty months later Nancy gave birth to a baby boy we named Ryan, and he was the reverse of Alison's weight at seven pounds, ten ounces. He was much smaller looking after remembering Alison "walk out" of the delivery room. We now had a matched set and felt our family was complete. Both of our children had blond hair and were light complexioned.

Alison was an early walker and an early talker, but she had a great role model, too. We would read Cinderella to Alison over and over, and she soon had it memorized. When we put her to bed, we would try to skip pages to save time, but she wouldn't let us get by with it and would correct us by reciting what we left out. When she was only two, we would tell people she could read. We would tell them to turn to any page in Cinderella and just get her started with the first line. Alison would then finish the page verbatim as if she were reading. Both Alison and Ryan were very good kids, and although we had high expectations, they seldom disappointed us.

Ryan was an early walker, too. He didn't crawl much, but would walk crab style on his hands and feet touching the ground, but not his knees. We raised our children before political correctness of no play-pens, car seats, and all the other things parents have to do today. Alison and Ryan spent a great deal of time in their play pen and learned to entertain themselves for a long time. Nancy was a wonderful mother and spent a lot of one-on-one time with both of our children, but also needed some time to do other things in the house. We had a wind-up swing that Ryan spent a lot of time in. He really was content in it, but we have some pictures that make it look like he was left in it for days.

Alison and Dad in the "70"s

Ryan and Dad with longer hair

We would take bike rides with the kids on the back of our bikes, and put them in a flimsy bike seat with no helmet. We also took road trips in our "beautiful" station wagon with the kids free to play, fight, or sleep in the back area with no restraints whatsoever. Alison and Ryan can still remember the distinct smell of crayons melting in the window sills and a combination of various candies they had eaten all or part of on one of our trips. Some families look at these as dull, domestic years of their life, but I recall them as the best.

Nancy and I became active in the Boone Tennis Association, a group started by Milt Mattson and some other tennis enthusiasts in the late '60s. We had some social functions as well as tournaments for singles and doubles. Our kids were tennis orphans and had to entertain themselves while we played. We weren't the best, but also not the worst in our group, but it was fun and good exercise as well.

Our children were more programmed than we were as kids, but not as much as the children are in general today. Alison started dance classes at three years old and danced all the way through high school. She played softball for a few years, but it wasn't her favorite. Ryan also played ball starting in Little League at the age of eight. I have always been very competitive and helped Steve Duffy coach the second year Ryan played ball. I had to mellow some when I realized I was putting too much emphasis on winning. I was also from the "old school" of putting more emphasis on boys' sports than girls'. Alison became a very good athlete, but I should have spent more time helping her achieve her goals. I also made Ryan very competitive to a fault, as I am sure he wanted to please me by winning all the time. It is much easier to look back on flaws I had than to be objective at the time. Ryan excelled in all the sports he competed in and was the runner-up in the high school state tennis championship his sophomore year.

Ryan Grabau as a sophomore Iowa State High School
runner up in tennis.

I think Nancy deserves most of the credit for helping Alison
and Ryan become good students. They both became good readers,
and because of this, good students as well. We made the decision
together to send them to the Trinity Lutheran Parochial school, which
went from kindergarten through eighth grade. It was, and still is, a
very good school both academically and spiritually. The neat thing
about Trinity is that a student gets involved in many things that he
or she might not in a larger school. This included plays, leadership,
and even sports. It was a real family atmosphere, and I think both
kids have fond memories. When they got to the junior high years, it
may have been a little tougher to stay at Trinity because the classes
were pretty small. Some parents worry that their children won't be
as popular or not as good in sports or academics when they don't
attend a public school. We did not find this to be true at all. Some
of Alison's favorite teachers taught at Trinity. The school provided a
good foundation for their academic future. A parent always wants
their children to do better than they did and mine did. Both Alison
and Ryan graduated from college with double majors in four years,
Alison from Kansas University, and Ryan from Southern Methodist
University. Alison has gone on to get an MBA and Masters of
education and teaches seventh grade English. Ryan is living in
Elmhurst, Illinois and is Vice President of Client Development with
Citi Cards Partnership Group.

Nancy spent the better part of thirty-plus years teaching first
grade students. I really think she had, and still has, a special gift of
teaching. Children really liked her, and there are still young adults

that will tell her she was their favorite teacher. The thing that makes her such a wonderful teacher is that she genuinely cares about people, and especially her students. I am most definitely Nancy's most challenging student. She has been teaching me now for over forty years and still has a great deal to work on with me. Just when she thinks I have learned something, I mess up, and she has to work with me on the same subject matter over and over. These things include manners, patience, and thoughtfulness, just to name a few.

I want to share a few of the stories that have been told time and time again, but still make me laugh and cry. Nancy had a student by the name of Chucky who was a little overweight in first grade. Chucky's dad worked for our company, and he wasn't a bad worker, but wasn't dependable, and we had to let him go. One day Chucky was in the school office to be weighed by the nurse. Nancy was also there to pick up some paper when the nurse said, "Chucky, you need to watch how much you eat because you are gaining too much weight." Chucky replied, "I haven't eaten so good since Grabau fired my old man." Nancy was embarrassed because she was married to "Grabau." Chucky's story was sad because his dad and mother were alcoholics, and I can recall being called on Thanksgiving for money they said was for formula when Chucky was a baby. I told them I would go and get the formula for their little boy and give it to them. They weren't going to buy formula, but rather beer for themselves. Years later, long after his dad stopped working for our company, I heard his father had committed suicide. These stories are sad and tragic, and the kids don't stand a chance of success in life.

Another story on the lighter side happened when Nancy was working late at Garfield School, to get ready for the next day, and when she was ready to leave on this windy day, the door blew shut behind her catching her dress in the locked door. She didn't have a key, so she was faced with a dilemma: tear the dress to get loose or take the dress off to free her self. She looked in the school and saw the school custodian, but couldn't get his attention because he was vacuuming. She made the decision to take her skirt off and run around the school to the front door, so she could get back in and then retrieve her dress. She did have a slip on, so it wasn't as erotic as it might have been when she made her dash around the school. She was able to get back in the school, retrieve her dress, and get to her car without the custodian seeing her, we think.

Nancy won "Working Woman of the Year Award" in 1989, which she very much deserved. She truly is a "woman for all seasons" in being able to teach, raise children, be a wonderful wife, and still be active in the community in which she lives. If you want it done right, and with flair, you call Nancy. To tell of all the incredible times she has entertained would be another book. She has been often called the "Martha Stewart" of Boone because she entertains with such flair. We have put on showers for weddings and birthday parties, as well as theme parties just for fun. Did I mention what a good cook Nancy is? She is very creative, and loves to bake as well. One of her specialties is sugar cookies, but she also makes pumpkin bread and many other delicious items. She also loves *real flowers* as well as real Christmas trees, wreaths, and other decorations. She is an entertainment dinosaur in this fast paced world of fake everything, paper plates, and catered dining.

We are now grandparents, and Nancy loves it, all but the age thing. She loves to teach our grandchildren about manners, being grateful, and life in general. I hope they listen because she has so many wonderful things to share with them. Kids in general have always loved Nancy, so she is a natural with grandchildren. I have always loved children as well, and I do think this helps when you raise them. I don't know how many grandchildren we will be blessed with, but we will try to enjoy each and every one of them.

Nancy and I have been married now for almost forty-two years. Alison put together a "shutter-fly" book of pictures and a cute history of all our great years together. I love to look at it and wonder where the time has gone. Few couples are blessed with all the wonderful times we have had together, before, with, and after children. There are many things that make for a successful marriage. I think a common shared belief in Jesus Christ as our savior gives a good foundation to the marriage. I think the knowledge that we sin and need forgiveness both from God as well as our spouse is also important. A good sense of humor certainly helps, as well as some common interests. There is no one correct formula for everyone, but it has to be worked at; it doesn't just happen by chance. There aren't very many days I don't thank God for the wonderful relationship we have been blessed with. Nancy's brother Johnny once said we are like peanut butter and jelly, and you can guess who the sweet one is. I have been blessed throughout my life, but Nancy has been the greatest blessing of all.

TRAVEL

I HAD MENTIONED that as a family we had taken several road trips when I was young. We went south to Florida, east to Washington and New York, west to Colorado and Wyoming, and north to South Dakota and Canada. You can see I spent a great deal of time in a car when I was young. When I was just out of high school, my best friend, Fritz Westfall, asked if I would like to drive with him and his father to Mexico City to pick up his sister who was graduating from the University of Americas. I jumped at the chance to go on such an exciting trip. We drove in the Westfall's Studebaker with an early version of air-conditioning. Doc Westfall liked to drive and would pull as close as he could to semi-trailers to take advantage of the wind draft and get better mileage. By the time we reached Mexico City, my mouth was full of canker sores from nerves caused by being so close to the truck's bumpers. Years before, we would ride to the lake in the summer with Doc and his fifty-nine Chevrolet, at up to one hundred plus miles per hour. Fritz would tell me not to worry because it was a convertible and had a low center of gravity. We made it to Mexico City without mishap and saw some unusual things along the way. We stopped in a silver mining area and went down into a cave-like burial vault where the soil caused some of the dead bodies to mummify. There were several bodies that were very much like they were when they were buried. There were also stacks of skeletons of those that did not mummify. It was a great honor if your loved one turned into a mummy.

We also saw a family funeral with two larger caskets and several smaller ones. Doc was a good photographer, and he went to great length to get photos of the funeral. I had a little trouble with that. This was my first trip south of the border, and I was exposed to a different culture. It took a few days before we finally arrived in Mexico City. This was in 1963, and the city is much larger today. We had a great time at many different tourist attractions such as the "thieves market," the Pyramid of the Sun, and even the highest building in the western hemisphere.

The Pyramid of the Sun is even taller than the Egyptian Pyramids. The Westfalls had been to Mexico City many times, and we had pulled a small trailer down filled with items you might have trouble selling at a garage sale in the states. The Mexicans recognized Doc's car and came running. Doc opened up the trailer and began trading old girdles, blue jeans, lamps, and many other items for onyx chess sets, tin carvings, and other trinkets made in Mexico. We soon had a trailer full of gift type items rather than old clothes that we had hauled down. Fritz and I climbed to the top of the Pyramid and down before we left for more sights.

We went to a night club and thought we were big shots because we could drink mixed drinks there at our age without a fake ID. We saw two cute girls at a party and asked if we could be lined up for the next night. It was a Sunday when we took these girls out on the town. The drinking establishments were open even though it was Sunday, so we stopped and had a drink with the girls. They were cute but didn't speak English, and we didn't speak Spanish more than a greeting and thank you and good bye. Needless to say most of the conversation was between Fritz and I and the two girls with us trying to tell a few things by gesture or speaking English with a Spanish accent. My date didn't feel too well, or had too much to drink on an empty stomach and became sick. This wasn't much fun, and as I recall we ended the evening early, so much for our Mexican romance.

We had a long drive back to Iowa, but this trip did start a lifelong love affair with Mexico for me. I have traveled to Mexico many times since with Nancy, starting with the trip to Acapulco with her family the year before we were married. We even honeymooned there a year later. I will tell more about different places in Mexico later. The Westfalls became the founders of a program to bring medical help and financial aid to parts of Mexico, and the program was called "Partners of the Americas."

When my dad was about twenty-two, he took a trip out west in a model-T with his best friend, Fred Erbe. I had heard stories of some of his adventures and always thought this would be neat to do. Fritz

Westfall and I planned just such a trip between our freshman and sophomore years of college. Fritz's parents let us drive their Chevrolet Greenbrier van on the trip. Our plan was to drive out the northern route and come back the southern one. We put a mattress in the back to sleep on and were like the original hippies in 1964, except we had short hair. We drove to Cheyenne, Wyoming, the first day and spent the night there, going to the YMCA for a shower. We then were off to Salt Lake City, Utah, for the next night. We drove to the Great Salt Lake the next day to see how much salt there was and take a swim. We had to walk more than a football field to even get deep enough to float. There are no fish or any living creatures in the lake as far as I know. We took some pictures and went back to driving west. When our suits dried, they would stand up by themselves.

Our next stop was Reno, Nevada, "the littlest big city in the world." We tried to go in some of the casinos, but Fritz wasn't too sure of his fake ID, so if they asked, he would just head for the door. We drove next to Lake Tahoe, which was on the border of Nevada and California. It was beautiful, with a smell that was like fresh cut pine. The lake is very deep, dark blue, and extremely cold from snow melt off coming down the mountains. We spent the night there, and even went to a dance at some club with a band. The next day we rented small motorcycles and went for a ride on some of the trails near the lake. I wish we could have spent even more time at this beautiful spot.

We had to keep on our journey west, and we drove to a small town in California called Bridgeport when we had mechanical trouble with the Chevy van. We had to push the van to a Chevy dealer to find out that the rear end had gone out. They don't have these just sitting on the shelf and had to order one. Great! What would we do in the mean time in this little town? We called home to our parents, and Fritz's dad said to get the parts coming, and he would arrange payment. We did this and spent the day looking at bait and tackle shops, gun stores, and more bait and tackle shops. Someone told us to check out Carson City, Nevada, so we hitchhiked back there for a day. It was worth the trip, but I won't go into the details to protect the not so innocent. Next we thought we would go back to Tahoe for a few days because we had wanted more time there our first trip through. We were back on the side of the road in Bridgeport with a sign we had made on cardboard that said Tahoe. Rides don't come quick even for two good looking hunks that we thought we were. We finally made it back to Tahoe and were spending money faster than we had planned. We thought we could save some by staying on a beach where someone had left a lot of empty wine bottles. Do you know how cold it gets in the mountains at night even in the middle of August? We were so cold that in the early morning, we spent some of our trip money on a hotel room nearby to warm up and get some sleep.

The next day was just as beautiful as the last, and we decided to go to a nicer beach to sun and swim. We met a girl from LA that was there with her parents and made friends. They were nice to us and even took us water skiing. The water was very cold, but we had fun nevertheless. I think they gave us a ride back to Bridgeport because it was on their way home. We talked about some of the neat "cigar" boats we had seen on Tahoe with really big engines. We saw one pull into a dock that had *two* Mercury 440 horse engines with two four-barrel carburetors on each engine. It almost came out of the water each time those big engines turned over. The sound of those engines really impressed us. The man driving the boat told us his son had flipped a boat like this going ninety miles per hour. We didn't ask what the son's fate was. We were soon back in Bridgeport to see if the parts had come in to fix the van; they hadn't.

We thought if we were going to see the Pacific, we had better get there by other means. We ended up taking a bus to LA and changed our plans of seeing Yosemite, San Francisco, and Highway 1 down the California coast. We ended up in Santa Monica because we wanted to see the ocean and also try surfing. This was during the heydays of the Beach Boys, and we thought we were "beach boys." We rented two surf boards, got some wax, and gave it a try. Fritz and I were both high school swimmers, so that was not a problem. The waves there were not that big, so we didn't kill ourselves and had a great time trying to surf and waiting to "catch a wave."

We had been given the address of one of the girls that we met in Tahoe, so we called and asked for a tour of the LA area. She picked us up, and we spent the evening seeing the sights. We were then one day away from our bus trip back to check on the van again. We stayed down town in a bad area that last night, to be close to the bus depot the next morning. It was not the high rent district and not the smartest thing we did. The next day we were back on the bus and headed back to Bridgeport. We had shorts on and came back to some snow in the mountains when we arrived. The good news was the van was fixed; the bad news was Fritz's dad had a mild heart attack, and we needed to get home as soon as we could. We thought we would still drive back the southern route by way of Route 66 as the song goes. We headed out and drove long days and made it to Needles, California, when the rear end went out of the van *again*. We called home and Fritz's dad told us to leave the van to be repaired and ride the train back home. We even looked at some motorcycles as a way to ride home, but weren't able to convince our parents that this was a good idea.

We found a train station and bought a ticket that would take us back to Des Moines where our parents could pick us up. We were now very low on cash and did not have any credit cards that everyone seems to have today. We were now safely on a train and headed home. The train went through a part of Colorado that just happened to have a drinking age of eighteen. Because we were so low on funds, we thought it was a good idea to get off the train on a short stop and grab a beer and burger. We could see a spot very close to the station, and it would only take a minute or two. We ordered our beer and burger and waited, but before they were served, we could hear a train whistle. I said to Fritz, "is that our train?" Fritz said, "No, I don't think so." We ran out the door of the bar and headed for the train, which was just starting to head out of the station. We ran as fast as we could along side of the train, and Fritz grabbed a hold and jumped on a step. I was running, but couldn't make myself grab a hold for fear of being tossed under the train. I yelled to Fritz "I can't make it," and he jumped back on the pavement back to a full run and away from the train. This was being witnessed by the conductor, who signaled for the engineer to stop the train. We were then allowed to board and sat quietly while we were lectured on the danger of falling below a train wheel and getting dissected. We didn't get our burger or beer and used what little money we had left to buy something to eat on the diner, which was more expensive. I don't recall anything else that was too eventful between Colorado and Des Moines. We were picked up by my parents in Des Moines and had a lot of good memories, but not much money left from our trip.

I mentioned that when I was young, I took several road trips with my parents. I tried to keep track of the states I had been in and continued to do this even today. If my memory serves me right, I have been in every state except Idaho, Montana, and Alaska. I was reading some obituaries that I found in a trunk in the attic and came across one of Herbert Grabau, who was a cousin to my dad. Herbert had taught science in Des Moines at Lincoln High School. He was married to Molly, and they were a rather eccentric couple. When Herbert and Molly would come to visit, he would often bring a snake or some unusual animal with him. One time he brought a bull snake to help eat rodents that might be near corn cribs near our house. We made the mistake of telling my mother, who was scared to death of snakes, and she said she would not come out of the house until it was caught. I kind of enjoyed the unusual animals, but he stopped bringing them after that episode. I'm sorry to digress;

the thing I was impressed by in the obituary was that Herbert had traveled to every state, including Alaska and Hawaii. He had been to every continent except Australia and had a very extensive resume of travel destinations. I think I always had a love for travel and to see what was over the next hill, but even with the love of travel, I always look forward to coming home. I think travel takes a person a little out of your comfort zone and makes you learn some new things such as a new culture, how to use other modes of transportation, or just meeting more diverse people.

Most of the trips I have gone on have been with Nancy. It is so much more enjoyable if you have someone to share the trip with. We have done a number of trips in the United States, and I can't remember a bad one. One of our first ones after Acapulco on our honeymoon included The Hemisphere in San Antonio, Texas. This was when we lived in Fort Worth, so we drove down. I had never seen the Alamo in person, and it is really just the front of the old church that is left now in the middle of the city.

We have gone to Colorado many times and skied a few times, too. I love the mountains both in the winter and summer. Nancy doesn't like the cold as well as the warm weather, so I have been skiing a few times with the guys. My daughter calls this "male pattern bonding." I went several times with friends from Boone and Ames staying in Breckenridge and Keystone. After doing this several years, the group fell apart, and I became a ski orphan and was adopted by some of the MBI staff and members. Jim Ryan had been the Executive

Secretary of the MBI and then took a job with a contractor in Des Moines called Taylor Ball. His boss, Jack Taylor, owned a place at the Keystone ranch just outside of Keystone that he would let his employees use for one hundred dollars a day to take care of cleanup. The place was a beautiful, log cabin-style with six bedrooms, a dorm room, a beautiful kitchen, and even a hot tub. It was built on a golf course because Jack was a golfer, but not a skier.

In 1989 Nancy's family had a reunion in Colorado Springs. Just about her whole family came. The central meeting place for the reunion was at her cousin's home, which is very close to the Broadmoor Hotel. It was two years after Nancy's grandmother, who we called Gigi, passed away. She had always liked when the whole family would get together, and this was to honor her memory. We had each family do a skit to entertain the rest of the group, and everyone had a good laugh.

Nancy's brother Jim liked to do something a little more adventuresome, so he asked who would like to climb Pikes Peak. Ryan, Alison, and I were up for it as were Buddy (Nancy's brother-in-law, married to Gail), Leslie (Jim's wife), and Johnny (Nancy's brother), and his wife, Julie.

We set out in the morning to a parking lot located near some "crags" to start our climb. The whole ride to this starting spot, Julie bragged about what a great climber she was. She said "I don't know about Johnny, but I have been climbing since I was knee high to a grasshopper." We all just listened, and I thought of a saying I had heard when I was younger, "Don't brag, and you won't have anything to live up to!" We parked the car and started our climb. It was just a trail and not a difficult climb, but we were apprehensive because Susan's husband, Clyde, a pulmonary doctor, had told us that flatlanders such as us would have trouble with the altitude. We were only a hundred yards or so from the car when Julie, "the mountain goat," said "My feet are killing me, and I'm going back to the car to wait!" Johnny said, "Is it okay if I hike to the timber line and then come back and wait with you?" Julie said, "Sure, but don't be too long!"

The day was clear and cool as we hiked upward. The view just kept getting better as we went up the trail. I did fine until about the last five hundred yards when breathing became much tougher as we were close to fourteen thousand feet above sea level. This was the first "14" I had climbed, and it was a great feeling when we reached the top. The only thing about Pikes Peak is the several hundred others had also reached the summit by riding a bus or driving their car. It was about sixty degrees and clear when we first reached the top.

I had been on top of Pike's Peak with my dad on a trip out west when I was about seven. We had ridden up on a cable car when a fog moved in, and everyone was trying to find a way back down because you couldn't see anything in the fog. The cable car was full, so we ended up taking a Model A down on the snake-like dirt road with very little visibility. The road down was a cork screw with very little room for error. I recall being very glad to be down and out of the fog.

I needed to catch my breath when the sky suddenly turned grey and large snowflakes started to fall on the mountain top. We sent Jim and Ryan down for the car and then tried to find a ride back down for ourselves. We found a van with two people who said they could drive us down to the car. We arrived to find Julie and Johnny in another car eating snacks while they waited for us. Jim Pennington and Ryan arrived soon, and we concluded our mountain adventure.

When I was twenty-eight and had two children and a lovely wife, I was asked by a local banker if I would consider applying for a place on the Rotary Group Study Team that would be forming. The trip would go to Australia and would be gone for over two months in the late winter of 1974. I was very excited and talked it over with my boss, Nancy, and my father, who was also my boss. They both agreed that it was a chance of a lifetime, and I should fill out the application. I did so and was then asked to come to an interview in Oskaloosa. I don't remember all the questions I was asked, but I think it went well. There were five team members selected with three from Iowa and two from Missouri. The team leader, Bill Lindbolm, was also from Missouri. Other members included Glen Kranzler, from Ames, Ken Puck, from Manning, Iowa, Don Birkeness, from Kansas City, and James Sayre, from Liberty, Missouri. We had a get-acquainted meeting in Bethany, Missouri, to meet each other and also finalize the plans. We were asked if we would like to come around the world on our way back for about two hundred dollars on our own. Everyone agreed that this should be done as the cost was so small compared to this chance to see some faraway places.

We arranged to have sport coats made that were dark blue and had some red and white by the pockets to make us look like the national table tennis team. We packed our suitcases and left on this adventure from the Kansas City airport on February 26, 1974, with our first stop Los Angeles, and then to Honolulu, Hawaii, for two days hardship lay over. This was also my first trip to Hawaii, and I really enjoyed it even though it was short. I tried surfing again, but had second thoughts when the board almost hit me in the head. I didn't want to cut my trip of a life time short by doing something really dumb. We were only on Oahu for about two days, but it gave us an overview of this beautiful island and a time to rest before our long flight to Australia. We took a dinner cruise on a sailing schooner that was a lot of fun. Our flight was scheduled to depart at 2:40 a.m. We flew British Airlines, and the plane was a 727, I think. The seats were close together, and we did not fly first or business class for extra comfort. We flew about six hours to the Fiji Islands to refuel. A day was lost at the International Date Line, and we landed in Sydney first and then on to Melbourne, Australia, to be greeted by the Rotary members. We were lodged in a motel and were able to swim and relax some before the evening dinner. I didn't realize how tired I was until we went out for supper. They offered us drinks at the restaurant, and we became acquainted with our hosts and ordered our meal. We talked, and talked, and talked some more. I noticed people from other tables come, eat, and leave while we had not yet been served. I asked the host next to me if he thought our order had been turned in. He said, "I'll check," and he motioned for the waitress to come over. "Excuse me, miss, but is our order nearly ready?" She felt in her pocket and got red in the face when she told him, "I forgot to turn it in." I was nearly asleep by then as we had some major "jet lag" by now. The dinner finally arrived, and we were glad to get back to the motel and catch up on sleep.

from left Don Birkeness, Rev. Bill Lindbloom, Jim in walking shorts,
Australian host, Jim Sayre, Glen Kranzler and Ken Puck

I can't possibly tell of everything that happened on the trip, but I will touch on some of the highlights and humorous stories I can remember. We kept dairies of the entire trip so now even thirty-five years later, I can see what went on that particular date. I wish I had done that on every trip so I would have a history of what we did and what we spent. When you look back over thirty years, even the cost of things can be interesting to compare to current times. We were given a booklet that had our entire itinerary for the eight weeks we would be in Australia. The country is divided into five states consisting of Victoria, New South Wales, Queensland, Northern Territory, Western Australia, and Tasmania. The group study was in the first two states I listed. We were to stay in one city or town about three days and then be transported to the next host town. We stayed in a few hotels, but for the most part we were in Rotarian homes. The first impression I got of the people was their friendly openness to us. It helped that this was a Rotary function, and they were told to show us the best time they could, but it went much further than just following orders. The opportunity to stay in homes is what made the trip so special. It allowed us to get to know the people and get a glimpse into their lives.

The tour was to start in the State of Victoria in the city of Melbourne and work northward into the southern part of New South Wales. I don't think I appreciated the scale of planning it took to put our tour together. Looking back, I realize what a commitment it was and what a great opportunity I had been given to participate.

My first stay with an Australian family was with the Reverend and Mrs. Roy Gabb and their four daughters. The girls were in their late teens and early twenties, the eldest being an elementary teacher. We saw some slides and talked about our families. The next day we were given an orientation and visited the Ford Motor Company. Rotarians in most countries throughout the world are the leaders of their communities, and this opened up a lot of doors for us to see things that others might not be able to. That evening the Gabb girls took me to see the "Moomba Festival," a celebration held in Melbourne. I saw a water ski show on the Murray River that featured barefoot skiers going seventy miles per hour.

We were most often treated to very special meals at all of our hosts, either at their homes or at a special restaurant they wanted to show off. Australia is an island continent, and most of the population is on the areas near the sea. They have very good sea food, and we had the opportunity to sample a great deal of it. Our hosts took us to a restaurant called the "Bird and Bottle" for a dinner of lobster and wine. The lobster is the spiny African variety, without large claws. Australia is also known for their fine wines, and we also tasted many of them in our travels as well. Early in our trip I suggested we have a bet as to who would gain the most weight during our stay. We each agreed to a wager of five dollars to go to whoever gained the least on our stay in Australia. I, of course, thought because I was young and active, I had the best chance of winning; stay tuned to see who won.

We not only toured industry, but also were taken to wineries and breweries. Australian wine and beer were, and still are, regarded very highly worldwide. Their beer is heaver but tastes full bodied and is now available around the world. We toured Foaters and Courage breweries as well as Michelton and LIndermans Wineries. Many of the things were described as the largest in the southern hemisphere. At night we were able to see the Southern Cross, which is like the North Star consolation of the southern hemisphere. In the country I was amazed how clear the stars were in this beautiful country.

Our hosts had been told, by way of our bios, the things we enjoyed doing in our free time. We were taken to play tennis, water ski, and many other fun things. On one day we went to a river to ski, and this was a new experience for me. I skied slalom, and the boat was an inboard with a great deal of power. They asked if I liked to jump start as the river was only about four feet deep in places. Trying to act as if this were no big deal, I yelled back, "sure, that will be fine." They asked if I was ready, and I said OK when I had the ski on and was pointed in the right direction. The boat driver hit the gas lever, and I thought my arms were going to come out of their sockets. Needless to say, I didn't get up the first time I tried. I told them when they turned back around that I had better go back to my old way of being in a sit down position to come out of the water. The second time worked much better, and I came up out of the water with no problem. I really liked skiing on a river as it was smooth and very scenic. Skiing is a "show off type sport, and skiers like to do as many "tricks" as they know for those in the boat or on the shore. I was cutting across the wake and even doing some jumping as I crossed the wake. I wasn't a great skier, but was confident on one ski and wanted to look as good as possible for our hosts. I think I was doing pretty well when the driver decided he would turn the boat around and go the opposite direction back down the river. Did I mention that this was a narrow river? The inboard boat could turn on a dime, and it seemed that it was coming right back at me with one of us going up the river and the other down the river. In a lake the turns are wider, and a skier can control how fast he wants to take a turn by the arch he takes in the turn. If he wants to go fast, he stays way out, and his speed increases as he turns. It is a little like the game played on ice called crack the whip where the person on the outside is going much faster than the ones close to the "whip cracker." The trick in the river was to turn fast enough to avoid hitting the shore before you changed direction. I was learning this rule very fast as I headed towards the bank at speeds faster than the boat was going! I was able to make the 180 degree turn successfully and did not become a shore ornament in the process.

The other time we water skied in Australia was on a lake, which was very pretty, and a lot of fun. The host had a house boat that we used as entertainment central and then had a speed boat that we skied around the houseboat island. We ate and drank on the house boat and were able to ski as much as we wanted in between. Most, if not all, of the lakes in Australia are manmade. The vast areas of the country are dry and require a great deal of good water management to keep water in reserve for livestock as well as irrigation. A very sophisticated system they developed is called the "snowy mountain scheme." It is almost like perpetual motion in that they pipe water from reservoirs on the rainy side of the mountains to the dry side. The pipes are huge, and they route the water through electric turbines to generate hydro electric power on the way down the mountain. If there isn't need for the water at this time, they use the electric power to run pumps to take the water back up and recycle it. It is a very ingenious system and seems to work very well.

When I told people that it snowed in Iowa, they thought we must have mountains because they only get snow due to altitude. I assured them that we get a lot of snow and have no mountains in Iowa. All of our time wasn't just fun and games, and we were expected to speak at the local Rotary Clubs as we traveled around. Most of the time one or two of us would tell about ourselves, family, and job. There would be a question and answer period from those present and then on to our next tour or another meeting. Our team leader, Rev. Bill Lindblom, would use the same joke every time he spoke. We could judge what kind of audience we had by how his bad joke went over. I am not a great speaker, but I learned to feel at ease in front of an audience after speaking so many times. I can recall in junior high having to introduce an assembly speaker and being so nervous I could barely speak. Speaking is like anything else; the more you do it, the easier it becomes. I have learned that people like a little humor, and they seldom complain if you are on the side of brevity.

The Australians drive on the left side of the street, which takes a little getting used to. I only drove a little there, but enough to see that you have to think differently when on what we call the wrong side of the street. The nation's capital called Canberra was not on our itinerary, but Jim Sayre and I were given the opportunity to drive with someone that had business there for the day. We thought it would be a neat experience to see the government in action and compare it to our Washington DC. We spent the day looking around at government buildings, seeing some aborigines' protests, and just enjoy the beauty of the city. We were driven back that evening and got back on schedule the next day.

It is hard to remember all the wonderful times the Australian people showed us, but just paging through my diary, I can see we were treated very well. They wanted us to enjoy ourselves while we learned and made friends with people that live half a world away. We were wined and dined, as well as given the opportunity to golf, play tennis, swim, sail, and even learn to throw a boomerang. We went to a horse race one day that was at a small country track. One of our hosts was a vet and had to take a urine sample after each race to make sure the horse wasn't drugged. He would get the horse to "go" by whistling, and it seemed to work. He told us that the number two won more than most other numbers at the tracks. I bet two dollars on a horse with the number two and ended up winning eight dollars. I think that was the first and last time I have ever won something at a race track.

We went to an art show in Alexandra, Victoria, and I purchased a watercolor of Collins Street in Melbourne. We also got to go up into the mountains and see areas where they can ski in the winter. The mountains are beautiful and not very high. They showed us a cliff where two climbers had scaled, but because of its height, were unable to reach the top in one day. They rigged their hammocks on the side of the cliff and spent the night hanging about one thousand feet above the ground and finished their climb the next day. We even saw an overhang called pulpit rock that we tried to get Pastor Lindblom to pose on for us, but he wasn't too fond of heights.

The mountains are called "the Blue Dandenongs" because they are covered with eucalyptus trees that give off a bluish cast from a distance. These trees grow to be extremely tall with heights over two hundred feet. They have a unique smell that is good to breathe and makes the woods feel very fresh. There are also giant ferns that make certain areas very tropical with exotic birds, and I don't mean girls, as they call them in Australia.

When you travel even in the United States, you find words that mean different things from where you were raised. You also find different accents throughout the states, but especially in other countries. The Australian accent is a bit like a British accent with a southern drawl. They have many unique words that we learned and started to incorporate into our vocabularies. I mentioned that a "bird" is a girl, a "boot" is a car trunk, a "bloke" a man, and on and on. You don't want to say "You're stuffed" after dinner because it means you're pregnant in Australia. I made up a short story to illustrate some of these words when I returned and was asked to speak at a number of Rotary clubs in central Iowa. With movies and TV we are much more familiar with these little differences than we once were, but hearing them in person is still very interesting.

The eight weeks in Australia went quickly because we had such a full itinerary, but I still missed Nancy and Alison and Ryan. Nancy and I wrote every day, and there was a steady flow of mail that I looked forward to. This was and still is the longest time Nancy and I have ever been apart since we were married. I did very much miss my children, too. I enjoyed seeing other little children of my hosts, but it is not the same as holding your own. We had one other task to complete before we left, and that was to weigh in to see who had gained the most. The winner was Bill Lindblom, and I was the looser having gained the most. Well, it was worth it, and I never did regret eating all those good meals!

We had chosen to continue around the world on our way back home. The cost that we had to pay out of our pocket for the world air fare was very low. Our plane was to leave at 1:05 on Sunday afternoon to fly to Bangkok. We were given a farewell party on Saturday night in Sunbury just outside Melbourne. We had an experience of a lifetime, but were now ready to head home. A fog had moved in on Sunday afternoon, and our 747 plane was delayed in take off. We finally took off, but flew only a short way to Sydney where we were delayed another two hours. We finally were on our way at 4:00 p.m. headed for Hong Kong where we landed at 4:30 in the morning. I would have liked to see Hong Kong, but didn't know it would be on our way, so all I saw was the airport and sky line when we left for Bangkok. The plane arrived in Bangkok, Thailand, at six a.m. Monday morning. The whole group went together to Bangkok, and we even did the Rotary lunch and some tours just as we had for the last eight weeks. You might think after spending this much time together, we would be getting on each other's nerves, but we continued to get along well the entire trip. We spent the first day shopping and just taking in the sights. After a good night's rest, we went to the floating gardens on Tuesday as a group. People lived on the water way in small shacks with their waste and garbage just dumped in the same water they cook with and use for drinking water. The kids swim in the river as that is their play ground. There are long speed boats with open props that go up and down the water way. You may have seen these in a James Bond movie. We would stop and buy fruit such as bananas as we went up the river. The neat thing about travel is when you see places you have been in a movie or read about them in a book, you can identify with the place so well having experienced it firsthand.

That night we were invited to a ten course dinner at the home of John Reagan, who was a diplomat at the embassy. The dinner was incredible, and I wrote down all the courses in case anyone wants to hear them; I didn't think so. The next night we flew from Bangkok to Athens. The plane left at 7:15 p.m. for Greece with one stop in New Delia, India. Some of the team members got off in India to see the Taj Mahal; I decided to go on to Athens. The flight time between these faraway places always took many hours. When I flew over these remote areas of the world, it was rather daunting. I landed in Athens at 4:10 in the morning after flying all night. I remember landing in Abu Dhabi, United Arab Emirates to refuel, and men with machine guns were on the tarmac patrolling the area. The same thing was true in the Athens Airport the morning I landed. There was a message for me when I landed telling me that Don Birkeness and Jim Sayre were at a hotel and to take a taxi and meet them there. The hotel was clean and very inexpensive at four dollars per night.

We did some sightseeing, looked at the museums, and just wandered around. That night we ate shrimp and drank wine at a Greek restaurant; come to think of it, all the restaurants were Greek in Athens. We looked at the Acropolis at night as they light it with different color lights and tell of its history. The next day Don and I went on a day cruise to some small islands near Athens in the Mediterranean. The water was beautiful just as I had imagined. We stopped in Poros and Hydra, as I remember, and they were just like a movie with white washed buildings and fishing boats of bright colors near the shore. We played soccer with young boys and ate squid, hard bread, and drank red wine. It was a great day, and one I will never forget. I hope to take Nancy back there so we can enjoy it together.

Jim in front of Parthenon on Acropolis in Athens, Greece

The next day I left for Rome on a short flight after bidding farewell to my teammates that had chosen to go a different route back to the US of A. I arrived in Rome and took a cab to the area near the Coliseum where I found a "cheap" hotel, the kind with shared bathrooms. I walked to the forum and Coliseum and looked in awe at the history before me. I called a lady by the name of Mrs. Eva Dionisa, whose name I had been given by a young girl in Bangkok who was her sister. I knew no one in Rome and thought it would be nice to tell her I had met her sister. She was married to an airline pilot and said she and a friend would take me to a dinner spot with a floor show. They picked me up, and we had a good dinner and listened to an Italian comedy show, of which I understood very little. They dropped me off near my hotel, and I rang the buzzer to get in. A man came to the window and yelled to me with a frog like voice of someone that had lost his vocal cords that I was in the building in the next block. I apologized and went to the next block and found my room right where I had left it.

I thought that Sunday would be a good day to go and see the Pope, so I took a cab to the Vatican. In 1929 Vatican City was formed to end the secular tension between the State and the Church. It consisted of only 108 acres and about one thousand people. The Pope, of course, is the head of not only the city but the Catholic Church worldwide. I went into the Vatican and even went to church there, so to speak. I saw the "Pieta" of Michelangelo. It is a marble sculpture of Christ being held by Mary after his crucifixion. Michelangelo carved it when he was not yet twenty-five years old.

The undercroft of the huge cathedral is a crypt with many popes' tombs and other famous people that had the influence or money to be buried there. I wanted to see the Sistine Chapel also, but it wasn't open on Sunday, imagine that. I was greeted by the Pope along with thousands of others as we stood in the Basilica and watched and listened to him bless the crowd from his window high above. I think he said something in Italian like "would all you people please get off my lawn." I'm not sure those were his exact word, but I'm sure it's close.

The Rome experience was a little cold and rainy and, with no one to enjoy it with, was a little lonely. My final day was spent near the forum looking at ruins and thinking of Caesar and all the history I had read that took place here. In the states we think a hundred years is old, but I was walking among things that were two thousand years old. I also walked past the Vittoriano, also known as the "wedding cake." It is a large white marble building that looks like a wedding cake. It was built in 1885 to 1911 to commemorate the unity of Italy. I returned to Rome with Nancy thirty-some years later and enjoyed it so much more because I had someone to share it with.

I left for home on a Pan Am flight at 11:35 and was met by my sister who lived in Concord, Massachusetts, while Alan was a doctor in the Navy for two years. She gave me a tour of Concord, and I told her about my travels. The next morning I flew back home to reality. I was so glad to see Nancy and also Alison and Ryan. When we got to Boone, I went to pick up the kids, who were staying at Denny and Patsy Kollbaum's house. Alison ran into my arms and gave me a choke-hold hug. Ryan was not so sure he wanted much to do with me as he hadn't seen me in ten weeks, and he was only a year and a half old. It was so great to be a family again, and I had no desire to take long trips without Nancy again.

Most of the trips I have taken since Australia have been with Nancy or the whole family. Both Nancy and I love to be around water, so many of our travels have been to water or on the water. When Alison and Ryan were still pretty young, Nancy was given the opportunity to attend the Pi Beta Phi convention in Miami. It was only for a few days, so I suggested that I join her, and we would go down to the Cayman Islands and spend a few days since she was already close. I planned ahead and became a certified scuba diver through the YMCA so I could dive when we got down to the Caribbean. This was in 1975 or about a year after my Australian trip. I flew by myself through Chicago where I spent the night with Benny Vinzant, who was best man in our wedding. Benny was living in the Chicago area and working for a steel company as a sales person. That night we went to a movie that was a new release called "Jaws." It was scary, and the music followed me to my first dive in the Caribbean. I flew out the next morning and met Nancy at the Miami Airport to fly on to The Cayman Islands for a few days. We stayed on Seven Mile Beach in a town house that we rented. The water is that beautiful Caribbean aqua blue and as clear as Iowa drinking water. The island is surrounded by coral reefs and is a destination island for scuba divers near and far.

I lined up my first dive with a dive outfitter/guide by the name of Bob Sotas Diving. It was a two-dive trip, but since this was my first real open water dive, I only did the shallow dive, which was about forty feet. You would be paired with a "buddy diver to keep an eye on each other under water. The water was very clear and the coral, as the marine life, very colorful as well. There was a current that pushed away from the dive boat. It's best to swim into the current at first so when you run low on air, you will drift back towards the boat either below water or above when you are out of air. The women on a dive always seem to run out of air last and the men first. I think I used my air too fast, thinking I might not get the next breath if I don't take it soon enough. The main thing you must remember as you go down is to clear your ears to equalize the pressure on the descent. The other critical thing to remember is to blow air out as you come up and *do not hold your breath!* If you dive very deep, you have to plan your dive so you can decompress on the way up to avoid the "bends."

My first ocean water dive was a success, and it was great. We spent several days in Cayman, swimming, diving, and eating some great meals. There is a turtle farm on the island, and we took a tour of it. You could see the turtles from very small to full grown. The turtle is raised for meat to eat as well as jewelry from the shell. Wild turtles swim to shore and lay their eggs. If they survive, the baby turtles go back into the sea, and then adults return to the same beaches to lay their own eggs, and the cycle of life goes on.

I dove the "wall," which is the start of a sixteen hundred foot slit in the Caribbean. It drops straight off with a wall that is covered with coral, and when you look down, you see the deep blue of water that seems to have no bottom. I felt like they had a sound system that played the theme from "Jaws." I was just sure a big white shark was going to swim up from the abyss. Going deeper doesn't really let you see that much more, but it does increase the chances something can go wrong.

The Caribbean has been, and still is, one of our favorite places to vacation. The beautiful aqua-colored water is breathtaking, and all the islands seem to have that "Jimmy Buffett" runaway quality that is so refreshing when you really want to get away. We went to Jamaica with the Master Builders on one of the remote every four-year conventions. We loved it, and it was a neat way to get to know some of the MBI members better. I was able to dive again just off the shore in coral reefs that surrounded the island. We had such good memories of the place we stayed, food, etc., that we took Alison and Ryan back with us to the same spot a few years later. I can recall being down on the beach with Ryan when he was in about sixth grade and seeing a couple frolicking in the surf. Ryan came over to me and said, "Dad, I don't think they have any clothes on." I, of course, hadn't noticed until he mentioned it to me. We then read the sign that told us this was a nude optional beach.

We had a lot of fun with the kids on this trip as well as many other vacations we took together. I am sure this fed their lust for travel they still have. We saw a male dancer go under two Coke bottles with a limbo stick balanced between them. They would even do this with the sticks set on fire. We went to Dunn River Falls and did the obligatory climb up the falls. This can be seen in one of the Bond movies, I think. The older the kids get, the tougher it is to travel places like this because they become so involved in activities, or they would rather be with their friends rather than their parents.

Aruba was another MBI destination in the Caribbean that we participated in, years later. I remember the food being especially good and the desserts out of this world. The island is very windy and is not as lush as Jamaica. The water is very clear, and I dove a German ship that had been sunk during WWII. The ship is part way out of the water and only about sixty feet deep at the deepest point under the water. They have legalized gambling with casinos on the island, which was not a big deal for me since I gamble enough in the construction business. Early the morning we were leaving, we saw the infamous Larry Flint leaving the black jack table after playing all night. They told us he can win or lose as much as one million dollars in one sleepless night. Nancy went on a parasail ride while we were there, but said it was much rougher than she had experienced in Acapulco when she first tried it.

Nancy and I have gone on two sailing trips in the Caribbean. Both of them have been to the British Virgin Islands and both with Nancy's cousins, the Couffers. Ryan and Andrea came down for a few days the first time, and we all had a great time. My son Ryan worked for American Airlines when he graduated from Southern Methodist

University. He was able to get Nancy and me some sweet deals on airfare and we took full advantage of it. We flew into the island of Tortola, which is one of the larger of the BVIs. Ronnie and Julie had a partial ownership in a forty-six foot boat that was moored near Road Town on Tortola. We bought provisions to eat and snack on in the boat, even though we would eat our evening meal at some great restaurant on the islands. Nancy's cousin, Bob Couffer, and his wife, Jeanne, were with us, too, along with Ryan and Andrea, our son and daughter-in-law. The trip started with a total of eight people. The boat could sleep six comfortably, so one couple would get a room on shore each night. We sailed to Cooper Island the first day and spent the night there.

Ronnie, Julie, and I are certified divers, so we rented several tanks and gear to take with us for diving. We tried out our gear near Cooper Island the first night on a shallow dive. We then had a delicious dinner on shore and drank several drinks the locals call "pain killers." Nancy and I volunteered to stay on shore the first night in a little bungalow. We wanted Ryan and Andrea to have the experience of sleeping on the boat.

The next morning we ate breakfast on board and then set sail for Salt Island and the wreck of the Rhone, a mail ship that sunk in a storm in 1867. We put down anchor and went for a dive to explore the sunken ship. Those who didn't SCUBA snorkeled around the boat. We were teasing Nancy that these sharp teeth fish really liked red swimming suits, which she was wearing at the time. The dive was in about sixty feet of water, and there was a great deal of marine life living in or near the wreck. I got along fine, but must not have equalized properly because I broke a blood vessel in one eye. I had a bloodshot eye for a couple of days, but it was fine. Water pressure can put a lot of stress on your body the deeper you dive.

We then set sail for Virgin Gorda, our next over night, where we moored at Saba Rock. We could see Necker Island, a private island owned by the English businessman, Richard Branson, who owns a record company as well as an airline and many other business enterprises. Ryan and Andrea stayed on shore that night as they were going back the next day. That evening we had dinner on Saba Rock and were entertained by a tropical band and drank and danced into the evening. The trip became a little like the TV show "Survivor" as Ryan and Andrea had to leave us to go home.

That morning we sailed across to another mooring spot and then rented a van to drive to the "Baths" on the far side of the island. The Baths are a collection of huge boulders that are collected in this one spot, and you can walk in between them almost like caves with warm water trapped in certain areas, thus the name. We ate on the way back to the boat, at Spanish Town, and stopped to see Little Dix Bay as well.

On the way back to our boat, we had dinner at a little restaurant that was on a cliff overlooking the ocean near Savannah Bay. We spent the night on board and sailed further out in the open seas towards Jost Van Dyke for our next night's stop. I got to be at the helm for a while and really enjoyed it. It took us most of the day to reach Jost Van Dyke by late afternoon. We tied to a mooring rope, swam, and cleaned up for supper. Our showers were quick because the boat only has so much fresh water, and we didn't want to waste it. That night would be a special meal at Abe's where we would eat fresh lobster boiled over an open fire by Abe himself. These were African Lobsters, which don't have the huge claws, but the meat is still very sweet. We couldn't eat all of the lobster and took "doggie" bags for lobster rolls the next day. We had a few pain killers that night, and all was right with the world.

We took a walk up to the higher portion of the island where we could see for miles. There were goats on the hill sides near little huts where the native islanders lived. We could see St. John and St. Thomas in the distance, which are part of the U. S. Virgin Islands. We took a very short sail to Soper's Hole on the west side of Tortola to let Bob and Jeanne get a cab to take them to a resort hotel for a couple of days before going to Florida to spend part of the winter. After they were on their way, we were down to just four of us. We spent the evening at Soper's Hole and did some food shopping as well as looking in Pusser's, a well known watering hole, as well as unique gift and clothing shops throughout the islands. We ate some hot wings and had a relaxing time before going back to the boat to sleep.

The next day we sailed back to the north side of the island to Cane Garden Bay, one of the most beautiful bays and beaches in the islands, in my opinion. We went to the beach and watched the pelicans dive for small fish along the shore. They hit the water with such velocity, it's a wonder their eyes stay in their sockets. We suddenly decided it would be fun to see Bob and Jeanne's hotel and get a fresh shower while we were there. We found a cab and had the driver take us to the hotel on the opposite side of the island. We surprised them, took our shower, and they gave us a tour of their hotel. That night Nancy and I spent our last night on the boat as we had to fly home the next day.

We returned to the BVI's in 2008 as a celebration of our 40th anniversary of our marriage. We again sailed with Nancy's cousin, Bob, his wife Jeanne, and of course the owners of the sail boat, Julie and Ron. We started from Tortola as before and sailed a similar route. We spent one night at Cooper Island and then headed to Virgin Gorda and the North Sound where we moored at Biras Creek to spend the night and also watch the Super Bowl. We shared a table with a couple that were sailing for several months in the Caribbean and living on their boat. This actually sounds better than it is because it is a little like camping on the water. Don't get me wrong, it is very beautiful, but a warm shower isn't all bad once in a while, too.

The next day we sailed a long stretch to Jost Van Dyke. On the way we saw dolphins swimming a crisscross fashion off the bow of the boat. They swim with such speed and grace; it is a sight to see. Just like some seven years before, we ordered lobster for supper that evening. We took the dingy over to Sidney's for a "before dinner drink." They have an honor system where you fix your own drinks and keep track of what you drink and pay before you leave. We drank a pain killer or two and then went back to Abe's for our lobster. We were greeted by a young girl that was just a baby the first time we were there a few years back. We have pictures of her as a baby and then as a young lady.

The lobster was great again, and so were the pain killers. Ronnie had remembered the drinks being only three dollars or less at double bubble hour the last time he had been there, so he just kept saying "one more round," thinking we were getting such a good deal. When we got the bill, he realized that inflation had hit the islands, and the drinks were now seven dollars, and we had a larger bill to pay. We laughed so hard when we saw the look on Ron's face after ordering so many drinks for all of us.

The next morning we sailed back the way we had come to our next destination called Marina Cay, a very small island near Scrub Island and Beef Island, and also near the airport. There were a lot of boats moored there, and we were lucky to get a spot. Ron, Julie, and I took the dingy to Lee Bay and did a shallow dive since we had tanks with us. It wasn't a great dive but still fun to do something I so seldom get to experience. We returned to the boat and changed clothes for supper on shore. The food always tastes better when you have been in the water and have built up an appetite. After supper we went to the upper part of the island to listen to a singer/entertainer who was a lot of fun. He said that if someone in the crowd made a toast and ended it with an "rrr," to sound like a pirate, he would serve them a shot of rum for free. I had had just enough pain killer to loosen my lips and stimulate my imagination that I came up with this: "With lots of loving and lots of beers, I loved this woman for almost forty years, rrr!" It was worth two shots of rum for Nancy and me, which we both quickly drank to the loud cheers of all that were there. We all had a lot of fun that night before we turned in. Bob and Jeanne had a room ashore with an extra room they said someone could use. We tried to talk Ron and Julie into using it, but they said they had to stay with their boat, a proper response for "captains." We were then odd men in and enjoyed the night on shore.

After a good breakfast the next morning, we bid farewell for our next adventure to Peter Island and the rest of our fortieth anniversary celebration. We took a ferry to Tortola, then a cab to another ferry to Peter Island. We arrived in early afternoon to settle in and explore the island. Our room was very nice, very expensive, and had a great view. This was such a special occasion that we weren't going to worry about the cost for a few days. The island is private and owned by one of the founders of Amway, but no one tried to sell us anything or recruit us. The accommodations were all inclusive except for drinks. I must say the food was excellent, and there was plenty of it. One of our days we took a shuttle bus to the back side of the island, which had a long private beach with only about two other couples on it. You tell the driver what time you want to be picked up, and they return at that time. We played tennis in the morning and even did the spa thing one afternoon. It was very romantic and is a time we will not soon forget.

On our second to last evening, they had a special signup for a wine tasting dinner with a couple there to host it and explain the different wines as well as the pairings with the many courses.

I learned some things, and it was fun conversing with the other guests.

Like all good things, we had come to the end of our celebration on Peter Island and caught the ferry back to Tortola and then a cab to the airport. We had some extra time, so we took the little ferry over to Marina Cay for some lunch and to buy some trinkets from Pusser's Store. We then took the ferry back to the airport and waited for our flight home by way of Puerto Rico. The BVIs still remain one of my favorite memories of what paradise must be like.

Mexico was, and still is, one of my favorite vacation destinations. Some Americans don't like it because the people speak Spanish there, imagine that. I love it because it is another country, but close and easy to get there. My first memories were from that trip I described earlier with the Westfalls to Mexico City. I went again to Acapulco with Nancy and her family the year before we got married. Nancy's step-father was a pilot for Braniff Airlines, and we were able to stay where the pilots stay on lay over and use the pool and facilities at the El Presidente`. We had a lot of fun, and I roomed with Nancy's brothers. Nancy and I had dinner at the El Mirador where the cliff divers entertain by diving off tall cliffs into the ocean below for tips to be left in baskets when you leave the restaurant. It is very romantic, and I can still feel the excitement we shared to this day. The whole family took an excursion boat on a cruise around the bay. People on the boat would throw coins into the ocean, and local swimmers would dive to retrieve them with no masks or tanks.

We had so much fun that a year later we went to Acapulco on our honeymoon and stayed at a small hotel on the beach called Posada Del Sol. It was the first week in June, and there were not many guests. Nancy and I have been to Mexico many times since our honeymoon, and each one seems like another honeymoon. We took Alison and Ryan to Mexico for their first time in the early '90s. We had gone to Puerto Vallarta a couple of times on a recommendation from Susan Williams, Nancy's cousin. She told us of a place called La Jolla de Mismaloya, a hotel located in Mismaloya Bay south of the fishing village called Puerto Vallarta. This is near where they made the movie called "The Night of The Iguana," starring Richard Burton and Elizabeth Taylor. I think it has one of the most beautiful beaches, and it is on the edge of a jungle-like setting.

Just off the coast are rock formations called Los Arcos, a popular dive and snorkel spot. It is a stop for all the "Booze Cruises" and a very visible and beautiful landmark. The resort hotel has a beautiful pool with palm trees, in-pool bars, and flowers everywhere. There were two tennis courts as well as an area to rent kayaks and other water sport equipment. The hotel was a twenty-minute bus ride to the downtown area. The bus is an experience in itself with workers and tourists riding side by side. I liked the experience of seeing the local Mexican people as if we lived there full time. The downtown is an old fishing village with the unique charm of shops, restaurants, and a setting right on the bay. We have several favorite restaurants that we have frequented over the years. They include La Bistro, El Set, for beautiful sunsets and great margaritas, and Porto Bella for excellent Italian cuisine located in "La Marina." There are many excellent restaurants, and we eat more "Mexican food" in the U.S. than we do in Mexico.

Cabo San Lucas is another of our favorite destinations in Mexico. It is located on the southern tip of the Baja Peninsula with rock formations that are called "lands end." We first went there in 1996 and stayed at The Westin Regina Resort on the Sea Of Cortes half way between Cabo and San Jose. The hotel has won many architectural awards and has many pools as well as many restaurants. It is a ways out, so you either have to rent a car or take a bus if you want to go into town.

We had a room with a "partial" ocean view, which made it a few dollars less per night, and we would joke that just seeing a part of the ocean was a major sacrifice. The hotel was beautiful, but a bit of a cruelty joke for the physically handicapped. It was built on the side of a small mountain, and there were many levels and lots of stairs. They had elevators, too, but it took several days to figure out which floor was which as they were so layered. The area is very desert-like, and the contrast between the deep blue Pacific and the sand and cactus added to the beauty. I went SCUBA diving in the Sea of Cortes, and it was fun, but not as clear as the Caribbean.

A few years later we had the opportunity to attend a MBI winter meeting held in Cabo. Nancy and I went down a couple of days early to extend the trip a little as well as have some fun by ourselves. We stayed at the Pueblo Bonito Rose with a view of "Lands End" at the southern end of the Sea of Cortes. It was the resort near where the

MBI would be staying in a few days. We ended up going to a time share presentation, something we had promised each other never to do again, and to make it worse, we bought a week. Looking back, it wasn't really a bad decision as we have had some great times since, both by ourselves and with the kids. We bought a "floating week" and can also book other vacations through RCI even though it is somewhat of a hassle.

When the MBI function started, we moved to the Melia for the balance of our stay. We had a lot of fun because the rest of the office staff joined Nancy and me, and this included Mary and Dick Youngblood and Eric and Julie Hammer. It was their first trip to Mexico, and I think they had a really fun time. I am not a big fisherman, but Cabo is noted for being one of the best big game fishing area in the world. They had an advanced signup for those who would like to try an outing. Eric, Dick, and I signed up, and we talked our bonding agent, Mark Keairnes, and Gale Rassmunson, another contractor from Sioux City, to go with us. We got up early and met at the Marina from where the fishing boats leave. There were several other boats besides ours that headed out to sea. We must have gone out some fifteen or twenty miles when the captain and helper put out large poles with lures to try to attract Marlin to hit or follow our boat. The first couple of hours were boring as we didn't see much activity. I started to read my book when we suddenly saw a fish jump in the area. The lure is replaced with a small fish to see if the marlin will grab a hold. It worked and soon we had a marlin on the line. I don't recall who had the first turn in the seat to work at landing this large fish. None of us were set on doing the whole landing by ourselves, so we each took fifteen-minute shifts fighting the marlin. I took some video of it jumping out of the water as it tried to get away. We had it just a few feet from the boat in about twenty minutes, and I thought this was pretty easy. Wrong! The rods have clutches on them, and when the fish takes off, the clutch lets it go so as to not break the line. The blue marlin got a second breath and was soon a long way from the boat. We each had a turn and finally broke the big guy's spirit, and it was now near the boat again. We really didn't want to keep the fish, but the boat captain asked if they could keep it, and we agreed to let them. The catch made the whole adventure worthwhile. We were given a beer as we headed back in to see if we had bragging rights over the other boats. The captain and his helper must have had hot dates that night because it was full speed ahead. We laughed so hard as drinking a beer in rough water was a real challenge. I recall stepping into the lower portion of the fishing boat just as we hit a wave, and I felt I was weightless as if in space when I should have been going down and was going up instead. We arrived back and got the obligatory picture of us standing next to our catch on the shore. The fish weighed in at one hundred eighty-two pounds, which was not a huge for a marlin, but was the largest fish any of us has ever caught. Many of the boats caught nothing, so we felt pretty good. This was one of the highlights of our trip. We had a feeling like Ernest Hemingway on one of his adventures, which reminds me that Nancy's grandmother, who we called Gigi, sat right behind Ernest Hemingway in grade school in Oak Park, Illinois, growing up.

182 lb Blue Marlin caught by
Dick Youngblood, Mark Keairnes, Gale Rassmuson,
Eric Hammer and me.

We have several favorite restaurants in the area that we frequent. They include Edith's, The Office, Morgan's in San Jose, and others. Anyone who says they don't like the food in Mexico must not have been to a Mexican resort area. There is even a very good sushi restaurant in Cabo called Nic San. Nancy and I have been back several times and stay at the Rose, Blanc, or at Sunset, all of which are part of the Pueblo Bonito group of resorts. This is really nice because you can go between any of these by way of shuttle and use any of their facilities. The area is also noted for incredible golf courses, but they are very expensive. I played with rented clubs on a course called Eldorado. I think the green fees were $250 plus club rental. My company bonding agent paid my green fees, so it was fun just to experience a course much like Pebble Beach in California.

Whale watching is a big deal in Mexico because the large mammals travel up and down the coast as they migrate south in the winter and back north for the summer. We have never taken a boat just for whale watching, but have seen many of them off the coast of Cabo as well as Puerto Vallarta. One time I was in Mismaloya Bay snorkeling when Nancy saw several whales breaching in the bay a few hundred yards out from me. She is shouting to get my attention while I am looking at little fish along the rocky coast. I finally see her and am able to look out and see a show the whales were putting on for all within sight. It looked like a mother and two cubs that were jumping or breaching in playful romp for our enjoyment. We have rented a condo from a Portland couple by the name of Jim and Embry Savage that sits high over the water on one side of the

Mismaloya Bay in Puerto Vallarta. We are able to look out from the balcony and watch the whales as they make their journey past. I try to bring binoculars and keep a look out for the spray as the whales spout when they come up for air. I also loved to sit and listen to the ocean break onto the rocks below in an explosive rhythm.

One other stop that we have spent some time at is Mazatlan, which is also near the sea of Cortes, but on the east side and further south. The Pueblo Bonito Resorts have two locations there, and we have stayed at each. The newer one is called Emerald Bay and is a few miles out of the fishing village. The other is closer to the town, and both are very nice. The downtown has a large indoor market that sells everything from fresh fish to butchered beef that is cut while you watch. Nancy and I walked by a refrigerated case that had a pig's head in it, and I asked her, "Would you like to eat this here or take it to go?" We were in the town center once, and they were having the "Miss Bimbo" pageant. There is an ice cream bar called Bimbo that sponsors the contest, thus the name.

We have had some great and relaxing times in Mexico. I think just being with the person you love in a beautiful place can't help but create great memories. We share the love of water, sun, (too much sometimes), and good food.

Alison & me on scuba dive off the coast of Puerto, Vallarta, Mexico

EUROPE

MY FIRST EXPOSURE to anything out of North America was my trip on the Rotary Exchange to Australia; when we came back around the world, I was able to see a little of Europe in Greece and Italy. I always wanted to bring Nancy back and experience it with her. Our daughter, Alison, applied for a study abroad program the second semester of her junior year in college. She was selected to study at the University of Sterling in Scotland. Alison always planned neat experiences for her summers between school years. She went to Finland one summer to spend time with a pen pal she had corresponded with since early grade school. She worked as a hostess for the Iroquois Hotel and restaurant on Mackinac Island, Michigan. These were not only ways to broaden her experiences, but she made some money as well. We didn't make it to Finland, but did go to Mackinac and Europe while she was in these places.

When Alison was in Scotland, we would look every day in the paper for special prices to fly to Europe. One morning we woke up and read in the travel section about a low price for a flight to Lisbon,

Portugal. We booked a flight, or should I say Nancy booked our flight, as she has on all our trips, and does a great job, I might add. Let me digress and tell a little of Alison's trip on her way to Scotland. I mentioned that Alison worked in Mackinac Island one summer, and while there she made friends with a girl named Sandrine from Paris, France. When she flew to Europe, her first destination was Paris with plans to see Sandrine on her first leg of her exploration of Europe before starting her second semester of her junior year of college. She flew all night and landed in Paris for her first day overseas. I'm sure she was tired, but they say to try not to sleep right away because you are trying to get your sleep clock on European time. She was traveling with a girl from K.U., and they stopped at The Cathedral of Notre Dame on their way to Sandrine's. While looking at the beautiful Cathedral, Alison heard a voice from behind her saying, "Alison." She turned around to see Linda and Jerry Bravard from Boone, who were on an anniversary trip to Paris. They both yelled with surprise to see a familiar face they weren't expecting and were asked to keep their voices down in the church.

Our contact with Alison came in alternating good call, bad call for the first week of her travel. She called us to let us know she had arrived safely and the funny story of seeing the Bravards when she first arrived. The next call wasn't as pleasant when Alison said, "Could you look on my bed and see if my traveler checks are there because I can't find them." They were, and Alison could do that American Express ad about lost or stolen traveler checks with Karl Malden. This wasn't a big deal as all she had to do was go to an American

Express office and get new ones. The next call was pleasant with her telling us about Paris and seeing Sandrine. She had purchased a Euro-pass for unlimited train travel while in Europe. They are expensive but a better buy if purchased in the USA before arriving in Europe. A pattern had developed, and I wasn't looking forward to her next call for fear it might not be good. It wasn't! Alison had been traveling on the train, and at a stop she had used a restroom somewhere in France, and her "security belt had been lost or stolen. This had her traveler checks, passport, as well as the Euro-pass. I had to let off some steam on my punching bag when I heard this. Alison grew up a lot on this trip and also whet her appetite for more travel. She learned how to get another passport from the American Embassy, how to report her loss to the French police, and not get too shook when unplanned things happen. A few months after she was in Scotland going to school, we received a letter from the French police department in Paris. Not being proficient in French after only one semester in high school, I took the letter to Jon Walczyk, who speaks and taught both French and Spanish to read and tell us what it said. He told us that the passport, Euro-rail pass, and miscellaneous other items had been turned in, and they wanted to know where to send them. I asked Jon to write them back and gave them Alison's address in Scotland. Most of the items had already been replaced, but the Euro-pass was worth finding and saved a lot of money not having to buy it again.

Let me get back to our trip to Portugal. We flew into Lisbon where we were to meet Alison. Europe is not as large as the USA, but this was a little like telling someone in Iowa to meet you in Texas when they are the one that has to travel a long ways to the meeting location. Alison is always up for adventure, so she didn't complain and got on the train in Scotland and headed south. We flew all night, as many of the overseas flights to Europe are overnight. The flight wasn't that full, so I laid down in a couple of empty seats on the other side of the isle from Nancy. The morning arrived, and I had gotten a little sleep, but besides that, I had gum all over my shorts that I was wearing. I had a hard time living that down.

This was before cell phones, so we just had to have faith that we would be able to time our meeting in Lisbon, and we did. We went to a nice restaurant to celebrate our getting together. I saw lobster on the menu and thought that would be nice. Alison and I ordered it while Nancy just had a salad. The bill came, and it was the equivalent of one hundred sixty-five dollars US. I think I got taken, but having just arrived, didn't want to make a scene, so I put it on my American Express and bit my tongue.

Portugal is a beautiful country with a great deal of history and a beautiful landscape. We stayed in some very unique accommodations called Posadas. These are old buildings that were convents, monasteries, or even castles that have been converted to places much like a bed and breakfast. Nancy had done some research and found out about these from a lady that used to live in Portugal. It made the trip so much more interesting than staying in a "motel six." It's hard to explain, but these old buildings take you back in time, and we are talking several centuries.

The people have a strong work ethic and are very friendly. We spent a short time in Lisbon and a little north of Lisbon to Obidos. We stayed in a former convent that was surrounded by stone walls for protection in years gone by. We went on to Sintra and toured an ancient castle. We had a rented car, and every day was an adventure. We didn't have a set itinerary, but did have accommodations reserved each night in different cities. We went to a "fair-like" celebration and ate cotton candy just like in the states. They also made cinnamon deep-fried bread, much like funnel cakes, which I recall was not healthy, but very tasty. One night was spent in an old castle up on a ridge of a hill looking down over a large valley. The wind was blowing so hard you could hear it whistle through the windows all night long. I can recall still feeling safe inside the thick stone walls and slept quite well in spite of the noise through the windows.

Our next destination was the Algarve, which is the very southern part of Portugal. It has beautiful beaches and is their vacation area. I asked how long a drive it was and was told, "It depends how fast you drive." The highways were good, but mostly two lanes with a shoulder on both sides. Our rental car was able to get up to about seventy going downhill with a tail wind. The BMWs and the Mercedes would pass us going about ninety. When a driver wanted to pass you, he would flash the lights, which was a signal for you to pull to the right and let him pass. There were often times when three cars were abreast on the two-lane highway. I will say you really paid attention to your driving because if you didn't, you wouldn't be around the next morning. I remember a car coming at us head on when Alison said "Dad! Aren't you on the right side of the road?" I said "Yes, but just not far enough on the right side of the road!" We made it in one piece and were to stay at a bed and breakfast out in the country. We had a little trouble finding it, but it was worth the effort.

Our hosts were Henry and Margaret Swain, who owned a home in the country with a beautiful swimming pool. The home was built of stone and was full of antiques and character that we fell in love with. Henry was English, and Margaret, Portuguese. Two other families were also staying there, which made for a real international flair. One couple had a little boy and were from Germany, and the other had a little girl and were from Belgium.

Alison was only with us one day in the Algarve region, so we drove to the beach to swim and get some sun. I had brought my mask, fins, and snorkel all the way from Iowa because I just knew I could do some snorkeling in the ocean off the southern coast of Portugal. I had looked at the travel logs and had seen the fantastic beaches and assumed the water was warm. Not! I would guess the water temperature was fifty-some degrees, and a wet suit would be in order. Alison did swim and came out with red blotches all over because of the cold water. The sand was a fine white, and the girls went topless, so all was not lost. We had a fun day at the beach and even saw some spear fishermen bring out some octopus from near the rocks.

Time had gone too fast, but it was time for Alison to leave to meet her traveling companion in Spain. We said our goodbyes and put her on the train. She was going to see some more of Europe before heading back to the states. We got to know the other couples as well as our hosts the next few days. Henry was a character, and he loved to ask questions about the United States. He would be cleaning the pool and stop by Nancy or me and say in an English accent, "That chap Reagan is a dandy isn't he?" He would then tell some story about our president from a different perspective.

The last night we decided to have a special barbeque with each couple bringing something for the evening's supper. The dinner was really good, and after our delicious meal, we played a game of trivial pursuit. I was Captain of one team and Henry the other. Now the game was the American version, so my team should have had some advantage, but we still lost, even though it was a close game. We had so much fun with this friendly competition and got to know this international group even better.

The next day we had to say our goodbyes and head back to Lisbon before going home. It amazes me how in such a short time people from different countries and backgrounds can bond and feel a kinship that makes parting sad. We drove back to Lisbon and caught a city celebration that was fun. The air was cool at night, and street vendors were selling fish on a stick much like the "everything" you get on a stick at the Iowa State Fair.

Our flight back was uneventful, but we arrived back to sad news. Ryan met us at the airport in Des Moines and told us that LaVern Condon, my head superintendent, had been in a bad accident and was in the Mercy Hospital in Des Moines in a coma. I stopped at the hospital to see him and told Dorothy, his wife, how sorry I was and that we would pray for him. LaVern was running a swine nutrition project on the west side of Ames at the time. He had slipped home to check on something and was headed back to the job on a gravel road just east of the industrial area in Boone when he was hit broadside by a car going south at a high rate of speed in an uncontrolled intersection. The impact was so hard that the other car was ripped in half, but the driver walked away unhurt. LaVern was in an unconscious state for about two months before he died. LaVern was a forty-some-year veteran of construction and had been with our company his entire career. He was sixty-five years old and really enjoyed working, but was also looking forward to kicking back someday. That someday never came.

ENGLAND

IN 1997 NANCY and I took our second trip abroad to England. As usual Nancy had done the research and had lined up some great places to stay and fun things to do. On the flight over I had head phones on and was reading about some adventure trip and said to Nancy in a voice loud enough that half the plane could hear, "I REALLY WANT TO GO ON AN ADVENTURE TRIP WITH THE KIDS SOMETIME!" A man sitting next to Nancy said, "I think you better let him go; he seems really excited." We flew all night and arrived in London early the next morning. Flying east you lose time the whole way, and it is never easy to sleep on the plane. We were very tired when we arrived, but didn't want to sleep and wake up in the middle of the night. We checked into a small but very nice boutique hotel and then went to look around. We got on a double-decker tour bus, and I was having trouble keeping my eyes open when the lady giving the tour said over the loud speaker, "I hope I'm not keeping you up!" I managed to keep my eyes open after that embarrassment. We finally got some sleep and were ready to rock and roll the next full day. We did many of the typical tourist things, which, of course, included shopping at Harrods Department Store, which is amazing even to me, a non-shopper. We saw the Tower of London, the Royal Guards, and London Bridge, as well as Big Ben. We had dinner at the oldest, continuous operating restaurant in London called "Rules." We even went to a play starring Jerry Lewis called "Damn Yankees."

We then headed north towards Scotland with our first stop Bath, England. Bath was given its name from Roman times when the area was noted for large bathing areas and was called the baths. We stayed at a small luxury hotel, The Homewood, that had beautiful gardens. We rode the train north to the Lake District where we stayed at the Linthwaite House Hotel, another small luxury hotel right next to the lake in the Windermere district. We took a ride on an excursion boat to see the lake up close. We spent time seeing Peter Rabbit and the Beatrice Potter books.

We soon were back on the train to Edinburgh, Scotland. What a beautiful city! We toured the castle and saw the men with their kilts and bag pipes. I know Nancy wanted to peek, but I wouldn't let her. We then went to a Scottish shop and purchased a kilt for Nancy since she is part Scottish and a member of the Clan Mackintosh, so she was told by her grandmother, Ruth Adam. When Gigi, as we called her, would visit Boone years ago and attend church with us, there would always be a sermon on our "sinful old Adam." When we left the church, I would introduce Gigi as "our sinful old Adam." I was probably the only one to think it was funny, but I kept using it any way.

We had a good time in Scotland and then rode the train back to London. Our stay in London coincided with the Wimbledon Tennis Tournament, so we thought we would take the "Tube," as they called the subway in England, out to see if we could get in. We had no tickets, but sometimes people leave, and they resell their tickets. It was raining, as it does quite often at Wimbledon, so we queued, as they say in jolly old England, or waited, as we say in the USA. We did this for several hours, and finally we were in the gate. It was still raining lightly, but we just wanted to look around and say we had been there. I bought Alison and Ryan t-shirts, got a program and a poster to take home, and we even ate some strawberries and cream, a famous treat at Wimbledon. We then went to the main center court to see what might be going on. We asked the military usher if it would be ok to sit in one of the box seats to see what it was like. It was still raining, and he saw no harm in letting us do that since no matches were on at the time. The court was covered with tarps, and we acted as if we belonged in the box seats with our umbrella and Nancy in her straw hat. We made friends with a British couple that had seats in the same box. It wasn't too long before the rain stopped and a little sun peaked out between the clouds. The time was after six in the evening, and they don't like to put men's matches on that late in case they might go five sets. The tarps were now being rolled back, so it looked like we were going to see some tennis. I whispered to Nancy to act as if we belonged in the box seats and just move over if someone came to our current seats. There were many empty seats around us, so I didn't think it would become a problem this late in the day.

The players were now warming up, and we were still making conversation with the nice couple we had become friends with. Just when I thought we were home free, I could see an usher headed in our direction with another couple to be seated. I told Nancy to just act as if we had sat in the wrong seats if they had the same seats we were in. It was a fool proof plan, until he asked to see our tickets. When I wasn't able to produce them, we were asked to leave, much to our embarrassment in front of our short lived friends. The story has a good ending though, as we were able to purchase tickets that had been turned back in and came back to the same match. They weren't box seats, but still very good, and we watched the match to its conclusion. The winner was Monica Seles.

Before we left London, I recall one more humorous story when we were waiting to ride the Tube. There would always be signs to "mind the gap" to make sure passengers watched the distance from the platform to the car, which would vary because of curves of the track, etc. Most stops just had a recording, but at one stop they had a man trying to keep passengers in an orderly fashion. He had a speaker, and before the train would arrive, he would tell those waiting, "Do not stand right in front of the car because those passengers getting off need room, and it will be much more organized if you wait further back to allow for an orderly transition." He said all of this with a very British accent and very seriously. The train would then arrive, and everyone would crowd to the door as if he had said nothing. When the train pulled out after total confusion, he would chastise the people still there by saying, "That simply won't do now; we must try harder next time!" The people he should have been talking to had already left the station. The other thing I remember is to make sure you look to the right before you step off the curb because they drive on the left side of the street, and you can become a "hood ornament" if you look the wrong way!

Germany

In 2000 we signed up for a group trip, something we have never done before. There is a city in Germany, called Oberammergau, that puts on The Passion Play every ten years. This has been done since 1634 as a thank offering to God for sparing this small hamlet from the Black Death, also known as the Black Plague, which spread through Europe and killed millions of people. The city had put itself under quarantine, and no one was to leave for fear the disease would be brought back. Legend blames a farmhand for bringing the pestilence back after working in a nearby estate and coming back to visit his family. Three hundred fifty people died in a very short time from his introducing the plague to the community. The elders of the village met and made a pledge to God that if the village would be spared, they would put on the Passion Play every ten years as a thank you. The story told is that after the pledge, no one else died, and they have done the play every ten years since. We were asked by Jan Miranda, a friend from Dallas, if we would like to go with a group from her church in Dallas, and we said yes. I will tell more about the play when I tell about Germany.

We signed up, paid a deposit, and planned our trip to start and end with just the two of us. Alison, our daughter, was getting her MBA from the University of Denver, so we wanted to see her graduate first before heading to Europe. We could fly into any city, so we chose Paris before meeting up with the group. Paris is all they say it is and more. We were only to be there a short time, but we saw a lot in two-plus days. We stayed in a small boutique-like hotel that was in the center of the city for easy access to all the sights. We went to the Louvre, the Cathedral of Notre Dame, the Musee d'Orsay, as well as the Eiffel Tower. We were able to take a boat down the Seine River and get on and off as often as we liked.

I took my video camera and captured a little of everything from French pastries to views from the Eiffel tower. We even called Sandrine and her "husband," Luke, and took them out to dinner. Sandrine was the friend Alison had met in Mackinac Island and had maintained the long distance friendship. After dinner they showed us all over the city, and every time Nancy would ask a question, they would answer by driving us to where something happened and tell us the story. Luke had to work the next day, but all he wanted to do was entertain us until way past midnight. The next day we caught a flight to Munich, Germany, to meet up with our tour group. We had a bus for our group tour, and it was nice not to have to worry about the driving. The tour stopped on the way to Oberammergau at a beautiful country church. These churches are very ornate and cost a great deal to maintain. We found out that a large portion of this upkeep is paid for by tax money, I guess, because it is for tourism as much or more than worship.

We arrived in Oberammergau later in the day, and a man dressed in lederhosen helped us with our bags. I think he had a crush on Nancy because she joked with him and is always so friendly. That evening we ate at the hotel restaurant, and who showed up to help serve the drinks but Hans, the man in the lederhosen. I think he had sampled a few of the beers all day long, too. When dinner was finished, a polka group played music, the polka, of course, and guess who wanted to dance with my wife? Hans was there with bells on to give Nancy a lap around the dance floor. The first round was fine as they did the polka and got a nice round of applause. Hans thought he needed an encore, so this time he put Nancy over his shoulder and danced one more time around the floor, much to Nancy's embarrassment. If you recall, this was a Lutheran church group we were with, and we saw a few eyebrows raised as he finally set her back down. We all had a good laugh, but Nancy kept her distance from Hans the rest of our stay there.

The next day we went to the Passion Play in the open air theater. It is all in German because, after all, we were in Germany. The play is six hours long and is very well done. They have three hours in the morning and the rest after lunch. The costumes were incredible, and the acting very good as well. I was thankful we had come over a couple of days early to recover from jet lag, or I would have been sleeping for most of the play. Some of our group had just arrived the day before, and I think their eyes were a little heavy by the time the play was over. Another thing that didn't help was the lunch we had was German dumplings, and these felt like rocks dropped in your stomach. I didn't eat much because I knew it would make for a long, uncomfortable afternoon. We knew the story line well enough that even though it was in German, we could follow rather well. I am glad we made the trip to see this incredible production put on by local people as a promise to God.

Tourism events bring a certain amount of commercialism, so the locals can make some money. The shops were full of books about the play, as well as all sorts of related items. Most of the shops were in good taste, and there was also an ample supply of cuckoo clocks for purchase. I elected to take home a short video that I took of the clocks doing their thing.

We went on to the Eagle' Nest, which was a refuge for Hitler, and also gave an incredible view of the surrounding country side. We went on to Austria, and finally Switzerland, to complete an incredible trip. In Switzerland we took a chair lift to one of the ski areas, and on the way up we could hear the cow bells from the dairy cows that graze the mountain during the summer. When we reached the top, the view was spectacular. There was a paraglider getting ready to jump also when we arrived. I got my video camera ready to capture the event. The jumper, who I found out later was a woman, ran and jumped off the mountain by letting the chute fill with air as she ran into the wind and then launched. My brain told me the jumper would start a slow descent down the side of the mountain, but I was mistaken. She went up as high as three thousand feet from where she jumped! Wow! Can you imagine if this were your first jump, and you thought you would drift down, but went up instead? She soared like an eagle to a much higher mountain across from us called the Eiger, made famous by a Clint Eastwood movie by the same name. I took video of her until she was out of sight. I later heard she landed in a village below the mountain several miles away. Our time with the group ended in Vitznau, a quaint little village on a lake below the mountains and sides. Nancy and I boarded a ferry to go across Lake Lucerne to catch a train to Lugano, Switzerland, to spend a couple of days by ourselves. What a great way to end our trip. Lugano is a lake also that was formed by the glaciers and is a beautiful setting. I swam in the lake, and it was a pleasant temperature. We stayed in a small luxury hotel called Grand Hotel Villa Castagnola. The hotel had incredible original art, and it was like being in an art museum. There was also a Ferrari Rally at our hotel, and it was fun to see that many neat cars all together. Switzerland is unique in that they have three different languages spoken in the same country, and it isn't that big. The people in the northern portion speak German, in the south they speak Italian, and near France they do as the French do. I was also amazed that they have palm trees in this part of Switzerland. Nancy and I had a wonderful time and would love to come back to this area maybe on the Italian side of the "Lake District."

ITALY

I MUST DIGRESS a little to explain how we went to Italy with a small group. It was several years before that we met a couple in Puerto Vallarta, Mexico, by the name of Dallas and Joe Bellio. We played some tennis with them and had dinner with them several times; when you are married to someone as outgoing as Nancy, it's not hard to meet people. Joe was a retired Delta pilot, and Dallas had been a flight attendant. Several months later they called us in Iowa and said they were going to visit some family in Ohio and wondered if we could get together? We said that would be great, and said we wanted them to stay with us. Joe had a small plane, and they were flying in from their home in Colorado. They spent the night, and we renewed our friendship. Our daughter, Alison, was married in 2003 in Denver, and we had kept up with Dallas and Joe telling them about the wedding and that we would like to touch base after the wedding. It turned out that they made a special effort to attend the wedding by catching a four a.m. flight from New York, where they had gone to see a play, just so as not to miss the event. We spent a night with them after the wedding and got to see their home. A year later they asked if we would like to join them and three other couples in Italy for a week. This became the catalyst to go to Italy.

Nancy and I flew into Rome and spent a couple of days there. I had stopped there on my way back from Australia, so I was a little familiar with things. It is so much more fun to have someone to share it with than to be by yourself, as I was the first time. We did the typical tourist things and saw the Colosseum, the Forum, and the Vatican. We knew that a sorority sister of Alison's was in Rome, but we had made no plans to meet her. We were tagging along with a tour group to learn a few things, unpaid, of course, and when we walked through the doors of the Vatican, who do we run into but Michelle and her sister, also touring the huge Roman Catholic Church. I told a priest back in Boone later that I was surprised that there wasn't a statue anywhere of Martin Luther to be found; he was catholic, wasn't he? Nancy and I walked up the narrow stairs all the way to the top of the Basilica and had a great view of Rome.

The old part of Rome was not built for automobiles, and the streets are really crowded. To cross the street can be a little challenging, especially the first step. The traffic will yield to pedestrians, but not until you start to cross the street. I had to almost drag Nancy to get her to make that first step. We rented a car to drive to Florence, and were glad to get out of the city. Italian drivers are good drivers, but they like to go fast. You have to be careful in the country because they like to cut the corners and may edge over to your side of the road.

We arrived to Florence without incident and found it to be a charming city. It is smaller and easy to get around by foot if you choose. There are many interesting bridges in Florence, with shops built right on both sides of the bridge itself. The shops are not full of junk or T-shirts, but rather really nice merchandise. The bridge is called Ponte Vecchio. We also got some culture by going to the Uffizi Gallery, an incredible art museum. There are so many master paintings that it is difficult to take it all in. We also saw the statue of David by Michelangelo in all its glory. When we were back in the states a friend of ours, Jim Gohman, took a picture of me at his home. A few days later we received a card in the mail with my head on "The Statue of David." The front of the card said "Nancy is a very lucky woman," and on the inside it said "to have married a man with a full head of hair."

We went back to our Hotel Roma, and the next day we drove to the central part of Tuscany to stay at Castello Di Velona, a small castle-like luxury hotel. It sat up on a hill overlooking vineyards and olive trees. You could see the poplars and cypresses that line the hillsides. We purchased a bottle or two of an award-winning virgin olive oil to take home.

The hotel had an outdoor pool that was a bit cool, but I swam a quick lap just to say I did. The next day we drove to Montalcino and then on to our meeting place, Montepulciano. One at a time the other couples arrived at the hotel they had selected as our home base. We got acquainted at a wine reception hosted by the Bellio's on their anniversary. All the couples were very nice and very well traveled. I liked the concept that we would go our own way in the day and then meet in the evenings for dinner and conversation. We would sometimes travel with another couple or even as the whole group, but never felt we were joined at the hip. We had several cars and could also take the train to different destinations. We visited some wonderful wineries and did the obligatory tasting too. One day several couples wanted to go into Florence on the train. Nancy was game for some more shopping and could also be a bit of a guide since we had been there once. I had always wanted to see the Leaning Tower of Pisa, as did another couple. We would ride into Florence and then take another train to Pisa and see the tower and return to Florence to meet the rest of the group. All went as planned, and we were soon on our way to Pisa. I told the other couple that I wanted to get a picture of the tower with myself in it for an ad when I got home saying our construction company could fix your building if it leaned like this one. We were about half way to Pisa when we heard a loud thud on the roof of our rail car that sounded like we hit a branch. The train rolled to a stop, and we could see emergency crews walking back and forth by our rail car yelling in Italian. In a little while we were escorted off the train to a small farm house. The electric contact arm of the train had fallen off, so they had radioed for busses to take us back to Florence. It was getting later, and I had told Nancy I would meet her at a café we had eaten at a few days before. I located a young girl that had a cell phone and also spoke English. I asked if she could call this café to tell my wife we would be late. She was very helpful, but no one would answer the phone. She finally called the Florence equivalent of our Chamber of Commerce to ask why no one answered the phone at the café. She was told the café was closed on Tuesdays, and guess what day it was? We finally arrived back at seven o'clock, and my dependable wife was waiting patiently near the restaurant that wasn't open. Our train made the evening news, but I don't think I did. It will take another trip for me to see the leaning tower of Pisa.

We took another day trip to a lake near where the film "Under the Tuscan Sun" was filmed. I think it makes films more interesting when you have been in the area where a film was made. Our group trip was coming to a conclusion, and we had one last goodbye dinner with great wine and conversation. The next day we drove back to Rome. You know what they say: all roads lead to Rome. It is amazing as you see road signs, and they all point and give the distance back to Roma. We spent one more night in Rome at a hotel that was safe and clean. I felt like we were in the witness protection program with our room having about five locks. We went out and ate pizza that night. They make up the "pies" in advance and then heat them up one piece at a time, almost as good as Belluci's. The next day we flew back home, only to arrive in the Des Moines airport with tornado warnings, flood alerts, as well as radio alerts on the way to Boone. We drove as far as Granger when Nancy said, "I think we better get a room and spend the night in Granger rather than risk not making it home." I, of course, just knew we could make it and was about to prove it! We drove to the Highway 17 turn off and started towards the river bridge. It was raining so hard I couldn't see the road and pulled over to the side. I came to my senses, and we went back to an American Inn and got their last room. We found potato chips in our bed, which led us to believe someone had a little employee party in our room before we got there. The next day we finally were able to drive home.

USA/CANADA

WE HAVE NEVER been on a bad trip and have had some great times in the good ole US of A. Nancy's brother lives in Hood River, Oregon, and what a great place to visit. Dr. Jim Pennington is a doctor by vocation and a mountain climber/bike racer by avocation. He always enjoys taking you out of your comfort zone when you visit. We go on some beautiful hikes and even some bike rides when we go there. We drove to the San Juan Islands and camped out near the ocean. The next morning we woke up to see a pod of Orca whales just off shore. Jimmy has climbed Mount Hood several times and was on the mountain when several climbers in another group fell into a crevasse and died.

Our all time favorite place to vacation has to be Lake Geneva, Wisconsin. Nancy asked her Great Uncle Bob Couffer, and Aunt Fran if she could bring me up for a week end the year before we were married. We have been back up now for forty-plus years, and they must like us because we keep getting invitations, and accept them. We always have a marvelous time and everyone takes turns with some of the cooking details. Bob and Jeanne own the home now, and their three daughters and families also enjoy the lake. Lake Geneva has been called the Newport of the west and is a playground for the wealthy of Chicago. The homes on the lake are incredible, both in size and design. A lake foot in 2009 sold for about twenty-five thousand dollars, so there aren't any properties under a million dollars.

Nancy's cousin's home has been in the family since 1925. It sits on the north shore just west of the narrows in a group of homes called Elgin Club, a home association that is well over one hundred years old. I think it is an interesting story how the "Elgin Club" came about. It seems that two fishermen were caught in a storm on the north shore. They survived the storm, but asked around if they could buy some property to build a cabin for refuge in a storm. They were told that a farmer had sixteen acres, but wanted to sell all. The two fishermen were from Elgin, Illinois, and bought the land for four hundred dollars. They returned home and asked others from Elgin if they would like a place at Lake Geneva? One thing led to another, and there are now eighteen homes and a caretaker's home on the property the fishermen bought. There is a small park behind with a tennis court and some playground equipment. The cabins have become large homes, and ownership has changed for some many times. The Couffers have been so generous to invite Nancy and me and our children up as well as their families. They have shared their boat, sail boat, jet-ski, and many delicious meals. Bob, a former mechanical engineer and graduate of Iowa State University, is retired now, and Jeanne, who once skated with the Ice Follies, is also retired from giving ice skating lessons. They now live on the lake year round except when they escape some cold for a trip south to Florida.

We should have purchased some property as an investment when we first started coming. The lake property just keeps going up in value. I don't know how I would like taking care of two properties, and we have had a great time all these years. The lake is very clean, and well over one hundred-feet deep in some places. It is shaped like a large boot and even has a golf course called Big Foot Country Club. It would take too long to describe all the fun times we have had on this lake and with the Couffers and their children. We have water skied, swam, played tennis, gone boating, sailed, taken excursion boats, built sand castles, and that was just the first day. If I had to describe my favorite part of summer, it would be two words, Lake Geneva.

I want to give one quick plug for Canada. We took a trip to Calgary in 2009 and rented a car to drive to Banff National Park. The Canadian Rockies are spectacular, to say the least. They are very rugged, and the upper portion, because of the latitude, is all above tree line. We spent a few days in Banff at the Fairmont in Banff Springs. The hotel is very grand and over a hundred years old. It is like a small city in itself. The region was opened up by William Cornelius Van Horne, the head of the Canadian Pacific Railroad, in the late 1800s. His famous quote was, "If we can't export the scenery, we'll import the tourists." The hotel is made of stone of a dark gray that gives it a very rugged exterior. It houses seven hundred rooms, several excellent restaurants, many shops, a saloon and salon, bowling alley, indoor and outdoor pool, an ice rink, and a spa, just to name a few. It sits in a magnificent mountain setting with the blue water of Spray River nearby. Not far from the hotel is the Banff hot springs, an original draw to the area. This is a natural hot spring thought to have healing water as well as a great place to relax with a slight smell of sulfur from deep in the mountain. We rode the gondola to one of the mountain tops for a spectacular view of the Canadian Rockies. We could see the Banff Springs Hotel as well as its golf course, one of the top courses in North America. A guest has opportunities to hike, swim, or just relax and enjoy the scenery. We hiked up a small mountain called Tunnel Mountain, a nice hike on a well-traveled trail. We started in the wrong place, and Nancy wasn't too happy with me because it was more difficult than it should have been. We had taken another hike on a less traveled trail, and Nancy kept hearing noises in the woods she thought might be a bear. I, of course, put her at ease by acting scared every time a branch would creek or a bird chirp. We finally made it to the "main" trail to the top of Tunnel Mountain and saw lots of hikers and no bears. When we reached the top of five thousand some feet, we were rewarded with a great view of our hotel, the town of Banff Springs, as well as the Bow River. We also were able to look up and see the steep northeast face of Mount Rundle another five thousand feet above us.

We spent three days in Banff Springs and then left for Lake Louise. The drive is spectacular in itself as the highway winds between the Canadian Rockies. We stopped at Lake Moraine on the way to Lake Louise. We walked from one end of the lake to the other and were amazed at the blue green color of the water caused by suspended minerals from the glacier melt that flow into the lake. We also saw signs warning people to hike in groups of four minimum to be safer if a bear was encountered. There are a fair number of black bears as well as grizzly bears that roam the park areas. They usually keep their distance, but, when they feel threatened, can become aggressive. The only wild life we saw was a few over fed chipmunks that would beg for food from the tourists. We needed to get off the beaten tracks to see more wild life, and it didn't seem to bother Nancy that we didn't.

We arrived at the Chateau Lake Louise in the late afternoon and found it was all we had heard about. The lake directly behind the hotel is also that blue green color with a glacier melting into the lake during the warmer seasons. We took a quick self-guided tour and then went out on canoe to explore the lake. We rented the last canoe to be allowed out at six in the evening. The lake looks larger in photos than it actually is. It is some two hundred and fifty feet deep, and the water is very cold. The water is clean, but you still can't see below the surface because of the suspended minerals in the water from the glacier. We were very careful not to tip over because of the cold, and we also carried cameras.

The next day we took a hike up the mountain that overlooks Lake Louise. Not only did we get a good work out but also a beautiful view of the lake, hotel, and the surrounding country side. There is a tea house towards the top, and we had some tea as well as some banana nut bread. I took a great number of pictures because every where I looked it was a great picture. That's a great thing about digital photography because you have an almost unlimited capacity to shoot and can save just the really good ones and erase the rest. We spent most of the day hiking, and Nancy spent it hiking and meeting people on the mountain from all over the world. We had a delicious dinner that night at one of the hotel restaurants.

The next morning we went into the town of Lake Louise to explore. We had breakfast at the Post Hotel that Nancy had discovered in her pre-trip research. The breakfast was very good and much like a farm breakfast with some refinement. Nancy had read that the hotel has a thirty-thousand-bottle wine cellar. I said you must mean three thousand bottles, don't you? She said no, it says thirty-two thousand on the review. This increased my interest because, although we aren't big wine drinkers, we do have a wine cellar with a couple of hundred bottles that we have stocked from wine club memberships. It also has become a room to display travel photos, so they don't look too obnoxious.

I asked the waitress if we could see the cellar, and she arranged for their wine steward to show it to us. The cellar has its entire walls, floor to ceiling, stocked with 2200 labels of different wines. She told us their most expensive wine is a French wine older than I am that sells for seven thousand dollars. That must be Canadian dollars, don't you think? They had a dinner table in the middle of the cellar to host wine tasting dinners. They even had radiant heaters to keep people from becoming chilled in the cool temperature-controlled room for the wine.

The next day we drove to what is called the ice fields. The drive is a little more than an hour, and the scenery on the way is breathtaking. We stopped to take some pictures at a lake that was just like a mirror. When I looked at the picture on my computer, it was so clear that it could be upside down and you wouldn't know it except evergreens don't grow upside down. We finally arrived at the ice fields, and if you wanted, you could pay forty dollars and a bus would take you onto the glacier and let you walk on the ice. This seemed a little high priced to walk on ice, even old ice, and we both agreed we get to walk on Iowa's mini-glaciers every winter. We did walk to the base of the glacier and could see how it has shrunk over the past one hundred years, a casualty of global warming, no doubt. We drove back to Lake Louise for a casual dinner and to pack for our trip back to Iowa. I love to travel, but I am always happy to get back home.

SPORTS

SINCE I WAS little, I have always been a little hyperactive. I had, and still have, a great deal of energy. My mother used to wrestle with me when I was young, and if she had me down, I would tell her I had to use the bathroom so she would let me up. My dad taught me how to play catch, and I think I had reasonably good eye-hand coordination. I never was given real lessons in any sport, but just tried to learn them myself by trying them and watching others. I did take swimming lessons, and as I mentioned earlier, learned to swim, but it took a bit longer to catch on about the breathing thing.

My first experience with any type of organized sport was Little League. I tried out and was "drafted" by the West Boone Dodgers. The glove I first had was so small, it looked like it was for ping-pong balls, or so some of the kids at school teased. I think I was on a Little League team either the first or second year it was organized in Boone. We started playing out in McHose Park, and then moved to a brand new field north of the tracks called Jimmy Archer Field. When the Little League program was first organized, there were only four teams, the Dodgers, Giants, Cardinals, and Cubs. There were no t-shirt teams, and the eight-year-olds played with the twelve-year-olds. I can recall we had a walking parade to the new park, and when I saw it, I felt like we were in the majors. I was scared to death the first time I went to bat against a twelve-year-old. I was nine my first year, and I think I played a little in the outfield, where players they wanted to hide usually ended up. I can remember Tom Magriff, who was a catcher for the Cubs, talking to me and telling me what to swing at. I would try to ignore him, but he would usually get in my head, and I would strike out. Each year I became a little more comfortable and eventually got to be a fair player. I played shortstop and wasn't a bad fielder. My hitting left something to be desired. I learned to bunt, and that raised my average some. Looking back I would have liked to have someone work with me to make me a better hitter. I was told that's what kept me off the all-star team when I was twelve.

The manager of the Dodgers was the Rev. Robert Stabenow. I can still hear his voice saying, "Choke up, Grabau, you're way behind it, now get a hit!" We had some nice kids on our team, and they included Marty Rinehart, Terry Sparks, Rick Metcalf, Ted Gifford, Leon Anderson, Bob Bush, Larry Sturtz, Joe Geyman, Dennis Reed, Raeford Bell, Steve Miller, Phil Gibbs, and Jon Struthers. We were one of the weaker teams at first, but moved up a couple notches when the league added two teams, the Tigers and the Braves. We had a lot of fun, and it really was a community event, with all the parents coming to cheer for their kids. I was always embarrassed when my parents came, and I'm not sure why. I guess I wanted to act older than I was.

The field was really kept nice and was a source of pride for the community. The infield was grass, base lines were chalked, and the outfield fence had advertising on each panel from stores around town. One sign said if you hit a home run over this sign, you get a free gallon of ice cream from Boone Dairy. A lot of lifelong friendships were forged on this little league field and some wonderful lessons were learned, too.

Young boys mature at different ages, and those that mature early have a physical advantage over those that mature later. We had a boy on our team named Rick Metcalf who was shaving before the games. I recall one game that he hit three home runs. I barely had to shave when I was a senior in high school. I do notice that the boys that mature early get all, or most, of their height early, and then stop growing. I was only 5'6" up until my sophomore year and then grew to be six feet by my first year in college. The girls always matured sooner, and it was a little intimidating to me.

The little league program really took off in Boone and all over the world. Boone now has a large complex with both boys' and girls' teams. There are t-shirt teams, minor teams, major teams, and the complex has many fields. Both my daughter, Alison, and my son, Ryan, played in the program. It is gratifying to see it come to this from those who got it started when I was young.

I went on to play Babe Ruth ball when I was thirteen. The same thing was true in Babe Ruth back then, and thirteen-year-olds played in the same league with the fifteen-year-olds. Now they have what is called a pony league for the thirteen-year-olds, and the fourteen-and fifteen-year-olds play in their own league. I was more confident than I had been my first year in little league, but still was a little intimidated by the older kids. I was put in at second base for my first playing experience in a Babe Ruth game, and a grounder was hit to me. I fielded it and was throwing it when the runner who had been on first ran me over and knocked the wind out of me. I survived and grew up a little that day.

I played short stop and second base and wasn't too bad a fielder. I was a better hitter, but could have used some coaching in this area to become even better. I wasn't afraid of the ball anymore and made good contact, but I think I would swing up and would tend to fly out rather than through the ball for a solid hit. I had a good arm and would play catch with whomever I could get to catch me. I think I really wanted to be a pitcher, but needed more control. I learned to throw a pretty good curve ball and found I could vary the curve by speed and spin. This would have been fine, but I found myself fielding a ball at short and throwing a curve to first base. Bob Herman was our first baseman, and the ball would move as much as six feet in that distance.

When I was fifteen, my interest in baseball had waned a little, and cars and girls were starting to occupy my mind. I was taking summer drivers education and would sometimes forget about ball practice, or be at ball practice and forget about drivers education. I was put on the bench a few times and was not used to this, and I showed it in my attitude. Looking back I sometimes wish I had kept playing baseball in high school because with some work I could have been a decent player. I did pitch some batting practice and had a strong arm. I was never put in to pitch a game because a manager has to have complete trust in the pitcher's control, and I don't think my coach did. Or he thought I might kill someone with a wild pitch.

I learned to shoot baskets in my parents' driveway when my dad put up a basketball hoop. We had a poured concrete drive, which, back then, was somewhat of a novelty. The Gustafson brothers would come over, and we had our own game with Doug and Mark taking on Steve and me. The drive is still there in 2009, but it looks a lot smaller than I thought it was back then. We would get kids from all over Boone to come out and play once in a while. The other place I used to go to play basketball was the YMCA. The Y was in an old building built in the early 1900s that was located on Eighth Street, across from where the Boone Hardware is now. The gym had a concrete floor and brick walls and was located in the basement. The Y had a pool, too, but it had been closed by the time I went there. There was a mixture of ages that would come down to play ball, and as a younger kid, you were thrilled to play with the older kids even if you didn't get to shoot much. The main floor had a game room with ping pong, or more properly called table tennis, at least two tables. They also had a game that we called hockey that you had to bank shots with a small piece of wood to try and make a checker-like puck go through a slot hidden behind a wooden peg. This taught me a physics lesson that HL would have been proud of, and that is that the angle of incidence is equal to the angle of reflection. When I got to seventh grade, I went to my first dance held every Friday night after the football games and thus the name, Grid. What a great time, and the junior high were on one floor, and the senior high on the other. They played fifties music because, guess what, it was the fifties, and these weren't "oldies"! I can recall asking a girl to dance and was amazed how soft girls' hands were. The last song was a real slow one, and you had to position yourself near the girl you hoped to walk home when it came on. We kept going to Grid even into senior high, and it's too bad they don't have it any more. The old Y is long gone, but it produced some pretty outstanding athletics over the years. I ran into a man that used to work the desk years ago by the name of Barry Wells, and he still remembered me by name. I didn't play basketball in high school because I was on the swim team. I did play some intramural and slow break at the new Y as a young adult. It's a great sport, and I gained an appreciation of the condition you need to be in to run the court the way they do now.

I mentioned earlier that I hadn't learned how to breathe when I did my trial swim at the Y-Camp. This was a setback in my swimming progress, but I did go on to become a fair swimmer. I loved to go to the Boone pool and swim, play keep away, and go off the boards all afternoon every day of the summer. This also was a social setting where a young boy could meet some of the fairer sex in a harmless environment. We knew the life guards, and when we were in junior high, they would let us go off the boards during the rest period and show off. Fritz Westfall, Rick Erickson, and I thought we were pretty cool. There were some days I couldn't swim because on game days for little league, we were supposed to save our energy. Those days we would just sit on the grass and play cards with the girls.

Most of my closer friends went out for swimming when we got to ninth grade and so did I. The Boone pool left a lot to be desired at that time. It's funny how time changes things. The Boone pool was one of the first high school pools built in the state. In fact the state swimming meet was held there the first year it was built in 1913 or 1914. I was a freshman in 1960, and the pool was getting pretty dated. It was twenty yards long, and the sprint freestyle was forty yards long. The districts were in Des Moines and held in a twenty-five-yard pool, so I felt we were at a disadvantage having worked out in a shorter pool all year. There was no age group swimming in Boone either, so as the late Charlie Cross would say to me years later "Jim, we were three month wonders and only swam during swim season." The pool wasn't very wide either, and the poor butterfly swimmers on the outside lanes had to be careful not to hook their arms on the steel ladders as they approached the end of the pool. I wasn't a diver despite all my practice and showing off at the outdoor summer pool. The high school pool had a beam that supported the first floor of the high school that was right in front of the board and none too high. I remember the Roosevelt diver warming up and hitting his feet on the beam while doing a full gainer and refused to dive in the meet.

I was a sprinter and had a pretty good thing going in that I swam the forty or fifty freestyle and was on both relays. I wasn't the fastest swimmer on the team, but those faster were faster in longer events, so the coach let me swim the sprints. When you are on the blocks, you hear the cheering, but once the gun went off, you couldn't hear anything until you touched at the finish of your race. I swam about a 19.7-second forty and about a 24-second fifty. I'm sure that with better training, weights, and year around training, these times could have been better. We had a lot of comradery, and swimming is great conditioning.

When I was an underclassman, the coach decided to have a contest to see how far we could swim under water. Most of us went two lengths under water or maybe a little further. Bill Cramer was our butterfly swimmer. He went a full three lengths and turned back on his fourth when he stopped and first came to the surface and then sank to the bottom. We thought he was just kidding until he didn't come up. The coach sent two teammates in to pull him out, and he was blue from lack of oxygen. The coach was just ready to give him mouth-to-mouth when he coughed and came to. It was a lesson learned, and we never had the underwater contest again.

I never qualified for state, but Charlie Cross did in both the fifty and one hundred freestyle. I had beaten Charlie only once in practice and that was after he had been sick. Our team was better than it had been, but still wasn't great. Mo Kelly used to drive a car full to some of the meets because he worked for the *Boone News* and also KWBG and would report on the meet. A few times we would take a school bus to the meets.

I swam one year in college for TCU. They were just starting their program and needed all the help they could get. We did beat Sam Houston, which made us all feel pretty good with such a small team.

I swam in the intramural meet the years I wasn't on the TCU team, and the Delts won first place, which was fun. Nancy and I still swim a quarter of a mile or better each noon during the summer to try to keep the weight off. Swimming has allowed me to learn how to do so many activities that I enjoy, and swimming is also an activity that Nancy and I have enjoyed together for over forty years.

Football was also a sport the Gustafson's and I would play together in the fall. I first went out for organized football in grade school where it was the flag variety. I played a lot of catch with my dad and friends and also went out in junior high. I was going through confirmation at the time, and that was held on Saturday mornings the same time junior high football games were. It was hard to participate when you knew you couldn't play in the games. In ninth grade I was already confirmed, so I was able to participate in the games. I was just ok, and not as comfortable in all the protective gear as I was just playing sand lot ball. Coach Morgan tried to make me a quarterback, but that didn't work out either. I played my sophomore year and thought I should be a running back, but my coaches moved me to guard, and that's where I stayed. I did get a letter that year, the first year you had to actually earn it and didn't just get for showing up. Most of my close friends didn't go out our junior year, so I didn't either. I sometimes regret not playing my junior and senior years because we had only about three or four seniors that played varsity from the class of '63. My son, Ryan, was a really good football player in high school and was the team's MVP all the years through high school except his senior year when he tore his ACL. He was small, but a tough kid, and played running back as well as defensive safety. I was the video guy, and I can remember Coach Merle Harris, a hall of fame coach from Boone, tell me "Your son is really hard to tackle." I said, "He is for his size." And Merle said, "No, I mean he is hard to bring down period." I thought that was a nice compliment from a coach that had seen a fair number of running backs.

I played intramural football for my frat in college and played end. I maybe could have been an end in high school, but it's a little late now. I have friends that still suffer some of the maladies from high school or college football, which have prevented them from playing other sports later in life. There are some things that I wouldn't trade for long gone "glory days."

I think it was in about seventh or eighth grade that I was given a tennis racquet for my birthday. I was never given instruction and can't even remember who taught me how to keep score. Fritz Westfall and I used to go out and play a few games, get hot, and then go swimming. I thought it was fun, but really never considered going out for the team. I wish now that I had been given some instruction because I would be a better player now. I played with a wood racket because that was the only choice back then. I played once in a while, but never took it too seriously.

When I went down to TCU my junior year of college, I took the racket with me and played a little down there. After college and after Nancy and I came back to live in Boone, we were asked to join the Boone Tennis Association. Milt Matson and several others had formed this association to have some social tennis as well as some tournaments. We had some fun times, and it became very successful with a lot of members. We also approached the Boone Park Board asking them if the courts could be upgraded. When we first came back to Boone in 1968, McHose Park had two courts with wire nets and a concrete surface. I asked the board if we could put up cloth nets, and they said that they wouldn't last. I finally talked them into letting the association buy the nets and put them up with their permission.

We worked hard, and two more courts were added as a memorial to a boy that had been killed on a motorcycle nearby. They weren't finished completely because they ran short of money. We had volunteers color coat the courts and paint the lines. Little by little the courts got better, and there are now six really nice courts at McHose, three at the DMACC campus, and two on the north side of Boone.

It was fun to watch the evolution of racquets because it happened just about the same time I became interested in playing more. The first racquet, other than a wood, was the T-2000, a steel racket that was used by Jimmy Conners, a very good pro at the time. I bought one, and it seemed like a lot better racquet than my old one. One bad thing about it was the sharp metal wire it had wrapped around the edge of the racquet that I would hit my leg with once in a while. From the T-2000 came the T-3000 and then a large assortment of all different shapes and sizes. Prince came out with an oversized racquet, and the body of racquets was made from all kinds of different material, from steel, aluminum, and even graphite.

This technology changed the game a great deal, and serves of the pros went up to one hundred plus miles per hour. My game improved, and I played some local tournaments, both singles and doubles. I was a fair server and would try to serve and volley, because my ground strokes weren't that good. I played a few times in the Storm Lake Tourney and also in Ames and Des Moines. I never became a great player but have really enjoyed the sport now for most of my adult life. Both of my children became tennis players and were very successful in summer Iowa Junior Tennis and later in high school. It is a sport for a life time and a good way to keep oneself young. I belong to the Ames Racquet and Fitness Club and play doubles two nights a week.

Tennis at Iowa Games

When Boone built a new Y, I played a little slow break basketball for a while and then got in a volleyball league. Grabau Construction sponsored a team for a year or so, and then I was asked to play for Eckstein's Diamonds. Now I must tell you that men's volleyball at the Y was a little weak on strict rules of how volleyball is played in high school or college. We were able to hit with an open hand and didn't always hit closed-fisted when hitting underhand. We had several competitive teams, and this made for some good matches during the winter season. We won the regular season a couple of times and the end-of-the-year tournament, too. Eckstein's team consisted of George Eckstein, Fred Grow, Denny Kollbaum, Arlis Mathis, Larry Briley, Carl Long, and me.

Y Volleyball Champs Carl Long, Jim, Fred Grow, Arlis Mathis,
Larry Briley, George Eckstein and Denny Kollbaum

When I was in junior high, Fritz Westfall's parents had a place up at Lake Okoboji. I went to the MBI summer meetings with my parents, and sometimes Fritz would invite me to stay at their lake spot on East Okoboji for a week afterwards. They had a cabin cruiser with a fifty-horsepower Evenrude outboard motor. This boat was heavy, and it took all fifty-horse, to get it moving. I was given my first water ski opportunity behind that boat. I don't remember how many tries it took, but I finally got up, and what a thrill! I skied a few times in high school when the opportunity presented itself, but never learned how to ski on one ski. I finally learned from a pledge brother how to drop a ski and then how to get up on one ski. There is something about learning something new that is very gratifying no matter what age you learn it.

I went to summer school one summer at TCU, and we spent a lot of time water skiing. We would go out in the morning and ski all day until the boat broke down or we ran out of light. The first boat that we skied behind was a forty-five-horse Mercury, and we could get two skiers on slalom up behind it. We would drag one leg to get the ski to plane out quicker, and it seemed we were under water for half the distance of the lake. Benny Vinzant's father owned the boat and let Benny take us skiing on Lake Dallas or any one of the manmade lakes near Dallas/Fort Worth. The boat I described would either run out of gas or breakdown by day's end, and we would have to be towed in to shore. Later that summer he traded it for an inboard/outboard, and that was really nice.

Our usual group consisted of Benny and whatever girl he had asked that week, Ross Brackett and date, Mike Newman, Carolyn Clemmons, and Nancy and me. Mike and Benny were the best skiers and would clown around after they got up. They would spray each other and cut back and forth and cross lines once in a while. One line was shorter than the other, and when the two skiers crossed, they had to make sure one line was high enough so as not to hit the front skier. Mike was such a strong skier, he would ski very rigid, and when he came across the wake would jump from one side to the other without touching the middle. He and Benny also would ski up next to each other, and Benny would hop off his ski and onto Mike's back, and Mike would carry him for some one hundred yards. This was over three hundred pounds on one ski, and all you could see was spray. I was able to learn how to get on Benny or Mike's back, but never tried the carry part.

We used to bring out milk containers with a small line and a weight tied to them and create a slalom course like you see on TV competition. Lake Dallas also has a ski jump that belonged to a ski club. It was usually locked up with a board across so people couldn't use it when the club wasn't there. One day when we were skiing, it wasn't locked up and so, guess what, we gave it a try. We didn't have the proper equipment and had no business trying the jump, but we were young and dumb. Ross Brackett was usually on two skies, so he was the "test pilot." We took a very slow pass so he could get his nerve up for the jump. The next time we came past, he started up the ramp and made it over and back down to the water. He went off it as slow as you could and still remain vertical. Everyone in the boat was laughing so hard we were crying. That was our only experience with the jumping, but I still laugh when I visualize Ross going off the ramp and the look on his face.

I bought my own slalom ski and thought I was really cool. I didn't have a boat so I would drag my ski around like "Linus" hoping someone would take me. I became a strong skier because if someone would take me, I skied no matter how rough the water was; wind, boats,, no problem, if someone was willing, I was going to ski! Both Nancy and I skied on our honeymoon, and it was a bit rough. We both skied at the same time, and when Nancy asked if there were sharks, the spotter in the boat said, "Si, don't fall!"

We would ski at Lake Geneva and any other chance we were given and finally bought a small Larson boat for our family when the kids were in about junior high. I remember one of the first times I tried the boat out was at Little Wall Lake, a small lake near Jewell, Iowa. When I was putting the boat in the lake, I had it all backed up and was now trying to push the boat off the trailer, and it just wouldn't budge when a guy with bib overalls fishing nearby, sitting in a chair on the dock, said in a country twang, "Might help if you undo the strap." I said, "Good idea. I was just making sure it was on tight." I felt like a fool as I did what he said, and the boat came off much easier. The boat was a seventeen-foot Larson outboard and just the right size to pull behind our car and fit our family into. Both kids learned to ski behind it, and we had a lot of fun. We kept it for about five years, and then the kids became young adults, and the boat was a little small.

After selling the boat, we went back to skiing once or twice a year until I bought another boat in 2009. It was a used Larson with an inboard/outboard and just a little larger, but I am still able to pull it behind a regular car. We took it to Lake Geneva and had a ball with the grand kids and our kids as well. Every year we can still get up on one ski is a great feeling. When you are young, you do things for the first time, but as you get older, you don't look forward to doing things the last time.

Jim on " fat boy" slalom 64 years and counting

Iowa is not the best place to learn how to snow ski. We have a few hills, but no mountains. I was given some snow skis when I was in high school and tried to teach myself how to ski. I think it much more difficult than water skiing. I read the book that came with the skis and learned how to slow down by pointing the tips of the skis in, or "snow plow." We used to ski behind the horse and also a car, which was a little more like water skiing, but the fall was a bit harder. Highway 30 south of Boone was in the process of being constructed at the time. In the winter it was a good place to pull a skier behind a car because it was just a wide-open dirt road with snow on it. Bret Downey had a VW, and he would pull me—and anyone else dumb enough—behind his car. I once was showing off, skiing behind my '60 Chevy with Tom Anderson driving and a girl in the car I wanted to impress. The car was on dry pavement, and I was on the shoulder of the road and kept putting my thumb up to signal for them to go faster. They reached nearly sixty miles per hour when I started to lose control and took a pretty good roll in the ditch. I only sprained a thumb, but I got a little smarter from the experience.

My first trip to Colorado was with Nancy not long after we were married. We drove out to Aspen to ski, and there were several people from Boone that had gone out, too. Denny and Sue Vaudt were there on their honeymoon, staying in a condo with George Eckstein and a girl friend. We stayed in a condo in a different location, and there was a Winnebago bus load of Boone guys out there as well. We skied a mountain that was geared for beginners called Buttermilk. It was a lot of fun and a good mountain for us to hone our lack of skill. We even saw the actor Lee Marvin on the top of the mountain. He didn't look like the tough guy he usually plays in the movies, but rather had on a powder blue snow suit and was smoking a cigarette held in a long holder. Bob Garvey, a friend I knew from Boone JC, gave us a quick lesson on things to work on, and it helped.

That night it was New Years Eve, and we all went out to dinner and then in and out of bars in Aspen. I recall Garvey being pushed into The Red Onion in a grocery cart they found in the street. He no sooner got in when a bouncer pushed him back out and dumped him in the street. The other funny thing I remember is that the water froze up in the guy's bus, so they would shower in Eckstein's and Vaudt's condo. Every day there would be a procession in and out of their condo of all the Boone guys. Nice way to spend your honeymoon.

New Years Day we skied again, and there was no one on the mountain in the morning, which was nice. I don't remember exactly the day we headed back, but we wanted to stop and see Vail. Nancy and I got to Vail and had fun looking around in the afternoon, but didn't ski there. We then headed for Denver late that afternoon—not a good idea. It became dark early and was snowing and blowing as well. This was before the Eisenhower tunnel was open, so we had to go over Loveland pass. It was white knuckles with several vehicles on the edge of the road stuck and our fear of going over the edge. We made it fine, but I was afraid our marriage wasn't going to for a while.

We went skiing again a couple of years later in Vail with just the two of us. We weren't much better skiers, but still had fun. I remember it snowing really hard one day, and we skied down a trail called "tourist trap." It got its name because it looks like an easy trail and then turns into a much steeper run with lots of moguls. We made it down, but part way was on our butts.

There was one day, I think our first, that we wanted to get every minute out of the day. We took the very last lift to the very top of the mountain for a long ski down. I thought I was doing pretty good when I fell, and my goggles cut the side of my nose, and I was bleeding all over my face. The ski patrol advised me I should ride down rather than ski. How embarrassing!

We drove back by way of Loveland and skied there, too, for a while. Nancy had a mishap and slipped getting off the chair lift and was under the lift with chairs going over her head and her legs pinned below her. They stopped the lift and helped her up. We both laugh at some of those times now.

We didn't take the kids skiing when they were young, probably because I was too cheap. By the time you buy clothes, rent equipment, and pay for lift tickets and lessons, you can go through a ton of money. Both Alison and Ryan have been out to ski on their own and can get down the mountain fine. Alison married Ben Pomerantz, a doctor by vocation, but a skier by avocation, and a former member of the medical ski patrol.

I didn't ski for a long time, but our tennis group talked about going out sometime for some "male pattern bonding." We finally called the bluff and set a date for our ski trip. The first time we went, we took the train out on a "red eye" special. We arrived in Denver early the next morning and then went on to Winter Park. Dan Lansing, Kirke Quinn, Ken Hampson, and I were on the trip. We skied for three days, which was all my body could take, but we had a great time. We rode the train back and played cards, read, and tried to sleep.

The next year we flew out to Denver and then rented a car to drive to the mountains. We went to Breckenridge the second year and then to Keystone the third. We would ski most of the day, take a steam bath or hot tub, and then go out to dinner. We would ski several areas in Summit County because they are all fairly close. I recall Kirke thinking he knew the way down a part of the mountain and ended on a black diamond slope covered with moguls. We laughed so hard we almost fell off the chair lift above him as he tried to stay vertical coming down the mountain. None of us were great skiers with Danny probably being the most experienced of the four of us.

My daughter, Alison, lived several years in Denver and came to say hi at the airport. She said we were so excited to get to the mountains, we barely gave her the time of day. Our escapades lasted for about four years and then fizzled out. I wanted to go out again, so I was talking to Jim Ryan, the MBI Executive Secretary and then Marketing Director for Taylor Ball, asking if I could go with their group. Jack Taylor had a beautiful home on the Keystone Ranch Golf Course and would let his employees use it for a small cleanup fee. Jim Ryan, Scott Norvell, Curtis McClain, and others all went out and stayed in this large log style home with hot tub and all. We did the same routine of skiing, eating, and drinking.

Alison and Dad at Keystone, Colorado

Alison even came up one day and skied and spent the night at our spot. The home had six bedrooms and a dorm room, too. Jack Taylor was a golfer, but it was very generous of him to let us use the place in the winter. I served on the MBI board with Jack, who was president of a very large construction company headquartered in Des Moines. Jack passed away a few years later from brain cancer at the age of only sixty.

I went out and skied a few times with just Alison while she lived there and also when she lived in Breckenridge. The first time I skied with her, she didn't want any advice from me and just wanted to be left alone. I went up with her anyway, and we skied down a green slope. She said that's kind of boring, and soon she was going down blue slopes. It wasn't too long, and she was skiing double black diamonds, just to say she could.

One last story before we get off the mountain. Nancy, Alison, and I were skiing Keystone one day when she lived in Breckenridge. Alison and I said we were going to ski one of the bowls, and Nancy was going to take a lesson. It started to snow really hard, and even Alison and I were separated for a while. We were to meet Nancy at the bar near the gondola we had started from at four o'clock. Alison and I went there, but found no Nancy. We had a beer or two or three, but still no Nancy. She finally arrived and told us she had skied to the wrong gondola and didn't realize it. She also told us that she had lost two instructors in the snow storm on her way down.

I joked to a classmate from high school at a class reunion golf outing that I was the best average athlete to come out of Boone.

The classmate was Roger Dutton, who is one of the best all around athletes to graduate from BHS. Roger played every sport Boone had to offer and played them all well. He went on to play two division one sports at the University of Northern Illinois, basketball and baseball. He was drafted by the New York Yankees and even was included in their expanded roster at the end of one year. He was playing ball on their farm league team and ran into the outfield wall breaking a bone in his spine that may have been hurt before while playing high school football. This ended his baseball career.

Roger and I were friends in junior high, but didn't do much together in high school. He came to his first class reunion twenty-five years after graduating. He hasn't missed one since, and we have become closer friends because of this. We even found out that we were both in the Marine Corps Reserve, and both Honor Men of our Platoons. I asked Roger at our twenty-fifth if he wanted to play some tennis. He said he couldn't because his knees were bad. "How about golf?" I asked. "No, my hip is bad, too, and it bothers me when I play golf." This is what I meant saying I was one of the best average athletes to come out of Boone, because I (knock on wood) can still do most of the activities I was ever able to do.

Roger had hip surgery and played golf with Mark Rasmus, Al Rasmus, and myself at our fortieth reunion. I had a better than average day and was low score with an eighty-six. I told the class that night at dinner that I finally found a sport I could beat Dutton at. I was joking, but when talking to Roger a few months after the reunion, he told me he wanted a return match. We played again at our forty-fifth, and I won, but I could see he had been working at his game and will no doubt pass me up by our fiftieth.

I started playing golf when I was in about sixth grade, but again was pretty much self taught by trial and error. Fritz Westfall and I would spend a fair amount of time playing at the Boone Golf and Country Club. It was a nine-hole course, so we would play the same nine over and over. The course was a little boring at times because it is pretty flat and predictable. That didn't mean that we shot good scores, even though we played it often. Some days we were just goofing off or looking for lost balls. It was the middle of the summer and hot when I waded into the number nine pond to look for lost balls. I was with Fritz, and he was getting ready to tee off on number nine. I said, "Go ahead and hit. I'll watch out for the ball." Fritz hit a line drive that came right at me. It happened so fast I guess I was mesmerized because I just stood there until the ball hit me in the head between my left eye and my temple. An inch one way or the other and I could have been blind in one eye, or worse yet, dead. I was knocked down in the reeds, and after a short while got up and cried. Fritz wasn't sure if he had killed me or what. I was taken to the hospital and got a few stitches. I did get a bit of a headache, but other than that was fine for the wear. I went out for golf a couple of years, but never was anything to write home about. I didn't play for a long time and then took it up again when I was about fifty-something. I can still hit the ball a long ways, but the direction varies depending on the day. We have a foursome that plays every Tuesday all summer, and it's a lot of fun. My only claim to fame was one Tuesday I got in a groove and had three birdies in a row. I also had an eagle during league play, which was a two on a par four. I have yet to get an ace, but there is still time, I hope.

Nancy had told me in college that she played golf, so we made a golf date, and I found out later that she had never held a club. Her grandmother had told her that boys liked girls that can do lots of things, so what's a little white lie. She spent the evening before our date learning all she could about golf for the next day. She lucked out because it rained all day, and we did something else.

Nancy started to play golf "again" about the same time I did. We would play together sometimes, but it can test your marriage. One day we were playing the back nine, and it was a beautiful day. We were just to tee off of number thirteen, but there was a flock of Canadian Geese in front of us. I told Nancy to hit a little to the left, and she would be fine. She hit straight into the geese and hit a goose in the side. It scared the geese back a little, but did no further harm. The ball, of course, stopped at the spot where it made contact with the goose. Her next shot was also straight at the geese, and this time she hit a goose in the head just above the eye in the temple. The goose went down on the spot and just laid there. We got in the cart and went to see if it was just dazed. The goose lifted its head and did a 360 and then fell dead with its legs straight up. Nancy felt bad, but there wasn't much I could do. At our class reunion I expounded on the story a little. I said that Nancy felt so bad she went to our Lutheran pastor and asked if he could do a memorial service for the deceased goose. Our pastor, Lindsey Watkins, said "We don't do those at our church, but the church up the street might be able to help you." Nancy said, "What should I offer them for such a service, about four hundred dollars?" Our pastor said, "Nancy, you didn't tell me the goose was Lutheran!"

I would like to have been really good at all the sports I play or have played, but I don't think you have to be a superstar to enjoy them. I don't have a memory of too many "glory days," but have had fun and comradeship playing many different sports, especially tennis and golf. I tell people I have moments of greatness, interrupted by hours of mediocrity.

Family portrait in back yard, Champ, Ryan, Nancy, Alison and me

MOTORIZED VEHICLES

IT MAY BE just a boy thing, but we tend to be obsessed with motorized vehicles from when we were very young. It starts with toys that we had to make the sound of the engine as we pushed them around the living room. When I learned to ride a bike, I would clothes-pin a card to the spokes so it sounded like it had an engine when I rode it. My first experience with a self propelled motorized vehicle was a scooter that I built myself with help from my dad and a local welding shop called Pesacks. It was along the lines of a "doodle bug," but with wheelbarrow wheels because they were cheap, and my dad, being in the construction business, had a bunch of them. I used a bike frame to start with and then, little by little, kept having steel pipes welded together until it looked like a small motor scooter. My friends, Fritz Westfall and Mark Rasmus, did the same thing, but we all had a little different design. They used the smaller typical "doodle bug" wheels on theirs. Next I had to find an engine that was to be the power source. I think my first engine was taken off some equipment that my dad let me have, and then later I bought a new Briggs & Stratton four-cycle engine of about six horsepower. I bought a centrifugal clutch that tightens the belt as it spins faster when the engine is revved up. This was really a good learning experience, although that was not my motivation at the time. Fritz and Mark used two-cycle engines similar to a chain saw engine. They were very loud, but faster than a four-cycle because they generated so many RPM.

I can't explain the excitement the first time the scooter actually ran, and I rode it for the first time. It gave me some independence that even the bike didn't seem to have. There was one obstacle, and that was we were only fourteen, and the law didn't allow permits for us to drive legally. Do you think that prevented us from riding? Not! We had to be rather clandestine as we navigated up and down alleys and on streets where we felt the eyes of the law wouldn't see or hear us. We were often having breakdowns and constantly modifying our scooters, but we felt like we were on top of the world.

We had the "bikes" out one night and were riding around when Fritz reached down to adjust his throttle and forgot the chain was there. He ran the end of his middle finger through the scooter's sprocket. It was still attached, but didn't look too good, and we got him home where his dad, a doctor, took him to the hospital and had it sewed back on. I think that was the last time he rode his scooter, and to add insult to injury, his old '50-something Mercury was stolen from in front of his house that night. Fritz turned sixteen and had purchased the Mercury just a month or so before that night. We were now all starting to dream about cars, so the scooters lost their appeal.

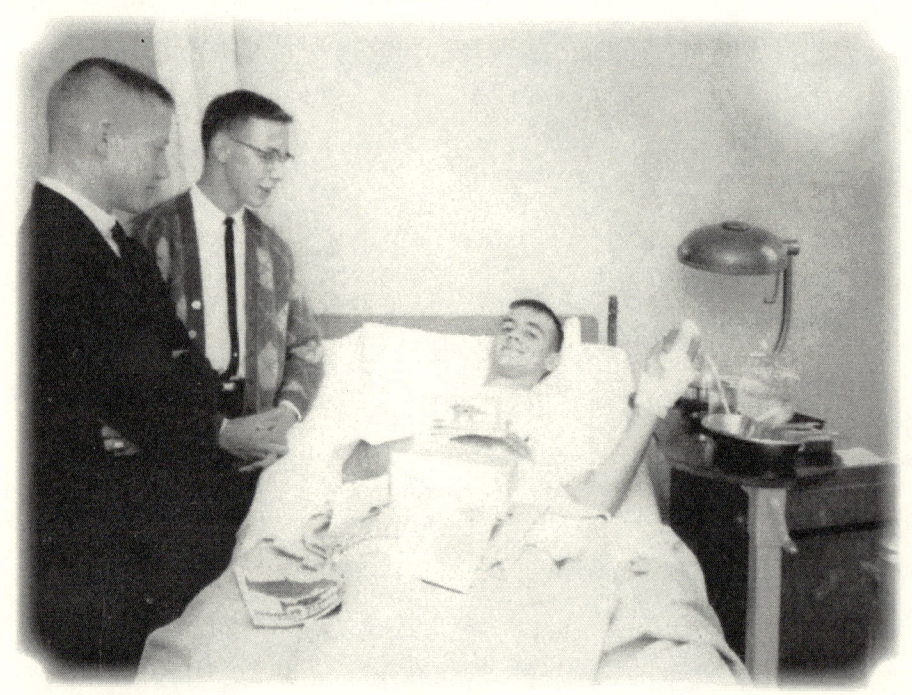

Jim, Mark Rasmus and Fritz Westfall at hospital after scooter mishap

My first experience with a four-wheeled vehicle was with one of my dad's old pickups in which he let me learn how to drive in a picked corn field. It was a three speed on the column, so I learned how to drive stick shift at the same time. My dad must have been pretty nice because we drove that pickup on the outer edge of the corn field like it was a race track, and he never complained.

I took drivers training in the summer when I was fourteen and then was allowed a permit to drive with my parents to gain experience. My dad traded cars for work about every two years because he put a lot of miles on them driving to and from jobs around the state. He had some nice cars, and his were always Chevrolets. He had a '57 two-door hardtop that was a turquoise blue, which would have been nice to keep. Some guy pulled out in front of my dad, and although no one was hurt, the car was totaled. He then bought a '58 Chevy two-door hardtop with a 283 V8 in a gold color. My mother also had nice cars, but they were all Oldsmobiles. They were usually four-door, but in '62 my dad bought a two-door hardtop for her with bucket seats and a three hundred horsepower engine. She looked like "the little old lady from Pasadena." I would on occasion "borrow" my parents' cars for test drives when they were gone somewhere with the other car. I was lucky I never was caught either by my parents or the police.

I turned sixteen the summer of 1961 and was at the door step of the court house to get my license the first day testers were there. I had already passed my written test and only had to take the driving portion, and like "Rain Man" thought I was a very good driver. I passed, and now at sixteen and a few days would be trusted on Iowa highways with a lethal machine. My dad was very generous with his car, and I had only to ask for the keys, and he always said yes. It was a Friday night, and we were "cruising the loop," honking at everyone we knew, which in Boone was everyone, when we saw another classmate who had also just been issued her license. It was Linda Coghlan out driving around with some other girls. They started to follow our car full of guys, and we got into a game of "ditch em." The object of this game is self explanatory and a little like the chases in the movies, but more controlled. I drove in and out of alleys trying to lose Linda, but she was hard to shake. All of a sudden as I looked in my rear view mirror, I realized there were three cars in the "game." The third one had these red flashing lights on top. We both got our first ticket and, of course, our names in the paper, so we would be ribbed by everyone at school.

I look back at some of the things I did and wonder how I made it to the age I am now. I was a little wild, but also under control most of the time. In 1962 I was riding around with a girl named Patty Jensen. We were downtown with my dad's '62 Chevy, a cream-colored, two-door hardtop with a 327 cubic inch engine and an automatic transmission. Gary Anderson, an upper classman, pulled up next to us in the passing lane and aced me out when the light turned green. Being very mature, I did the same thing to him at the next light. We did this for about three lights and were now heading south on Story Street at a fairly high rate of speed. Story had not been widened to a four-lane yet because the highway was not finished south of town. I was in the process of passing Gary when we approached the small hill just past where I live now and in front of where George and Becky Eckstein live now. The '62 Chevy was gaining on Gary's '57, and we were nearly side by side when I saw another car coming up the hill at me head on. I hit the brakes and went into a hard right skid, turning the car so I was sliding backwards towards the right hand curb. Gary floored his car so as to get out of the way. I slid up just over the parking and dented a wheel, letting the air out of one tire.

We were fortunate that no one got hurt, or worse yet, killed by that dumb stunt. Patty walked to a friend's house to spend the night, and I went home to tell my dad I had a "little" mishap with the car. Steve Duffy had to help me change the tire I was so shaken up.

My first car that my dad helped me buy was a red, two-door hardtop Chevy with a 283 V8 and a three-speed transmission with overdrive. It wasn't very fast, but was a really pretty car, and I washed it at least eight times a week. I had Hollwood-type mufflers that made the engine sound really kool, I thought. Gas was about twenty-five cents a gallon unless there was a gas war, and it dropped as low as fifteen cents. My car got almost twenty miles to the gallon if I used the over drive out on the highway. I was ahead of my time and had seat belts installed before they came stock in cars. I even gave seat belts to my mother for her birthday.

Our senior year Fritz, Mark Rasmus, and I built a hot rod of sorts. Mike Toot helped us with welding and parts recruitment. We found a '37 Plymouth and a '50 Ford and married the two into one car. We took the Ford body off and replaced it with the five window coop body of the Plymouth.

Fritz Westfall, Mark Rasmus and Jim with Plymoth-Ford hybred hot rod

The body came out flush with the Ford frame, but it didn't look too bad. We found the widest used tires we could and put them on the back to look like slicks. We didn't have all the proper lights, so we couldn't get a license and drove like we used to drive our scooters, under cover. We took it to the Des Moines dragway and the Iowa dragway in Humbolt and won trophies because no one else raced in C-Modified. Fritz drove it in Des Moines, and I drove it at Humbolt. The car was loud and had no muffler. When we were given the flag to start, the car would shake so much the flag man would run for cover for fear it might blow up. Drag strips were a bigger thing back then, and you could even drag street cars, which was better than racing on the streets. We ended up selling the rod, and I lost track of where it went.

Jim and Fritz with drag race trophy from Des Moines Dragway

My senior year my dad had a job in Centerville in southern Iowa and made a trade of my '60 Chevy for a 1965 Chevrolet Impala, red with a 327 cubic-inch engine and four-speed transmission. To tell the truth I think my dad was into the cars more than I was. This car had the three hundred horse engine and was pretty quick. It was raced a few times on back country roads, which wasn't the smartest thing to do. John Johnson, who went to Junior College with me, had an anniversary gold, '63 Chevy, and we would race once in a while. He had a three speed, and it would really whine before he would shift. My '65 was red, and it was the car I took down to TCU my junior year with no air conditioning. It had a black leather interior and really got hot in Texas. I had pledge brothers with really nice cars, too. Benny Vinzant drove a '65 GTO that I really liked. Steve Allison, my roommate, drove a '65 Olds 442 that was sweet, too.

When Nancy and I became engaged in 1968, my parents bought a new '68 Chevrolet for us as a wedding gift. I still look back in amazement all the nice things they did for me. I was driving this car back to TCU with John Johnson and Phil Seitz after spring break and stopped to have the break-in oil changed as they had told me to. We then headed back onto the interstate on a toll road and were driving about eighty miles per hour. When we went through the toll booth at the end of the turnpike, they told us the filling station that had changed my oil was trying to get a hold of me because they thought the oil plug was put back on incorrectly. The idiot light didn't come on because we were driving fast enough that the oil pressure warning didn't activate. When we stopped, the engine froze up immediately.

I was fortunate that the station was a national company and said they would pay for the damages and also a rental car while mine was being fixed. They put a new engine in the car and took care of all the expenses.

Ever since we built those scooters, I have always had a fascination with motorcycles. I purchased a 175 Honda endure-type cycle in my early twenties before we had children. I tried to do some hill climbing, but I really didn't know what I was doing. I went out to "killer" hill and tried to climb the fairly steep hill, but the front end would come too far off the ground, and I couldn't make it up the hill. Jerry "Buck" Monen was at the same hill and gave me some advice. He said you need to stand up on the pegs when you are climbing to keep weight over the front wheel. I tried that on the same hill, and it was amazing what a difference it made. The front wheel still came off the ground. but not so far and came right back down when I reached the top and went over the upper edge. I thought I was really something now!

I wanted a bike with a little more power, so I sold the Honda and bought a 250 cc Yamaha. It was used in a pearl white color and a two-cycle. I did some climbing with it and even went out and up some of the shale piles that were left from the soft coal days in Boone County. I was riding with George Eckstein one day, and we went to a small shale pile, and I was showing him what I had learned about climbing. I did fine the first time up and so did George. The second time I gave the bike a little too much gas and even on the pegs, my bike came over on top of me. I should have just left the bike go, but instead held on, and it fell over on my knee and popped it out of joint. It hurt badly, but I was able to get up and back on my bike and ride back to town. When I got off the bike, I could feel it wasn't very stable. I went to the doctor the next business day, and he told me I had hurt the ligaments on the side of my knee. It gave me some trouble when I didn't let it heal enough and tried to do some sports. When it would go out, it was not a good feeling, and I have had it drained several times. I have learned to favor it when I play tennis, and it has done well now for some time, knock on wood.

I sold the Yamaha when we started our family and didn't have a cycle for a long time. In about 1995 I purchased a 1960 BSA Royal Tourist Golden Flash from Baxter Cycle in a small town just off the interstate called Marne, Iowa. They have an inventory of British bikes including Triumphs and BSAs and all kinds of parts for these bikes as well. BSA stands for Birmingham Small Arms from a company in Great Britain that made small guns and expanded into motorcycles. A friend of mine, Dan Lansing, told me the BSA really stood for "the bastard stopped again." The bike was in good shape and had a 500cc twin cylinder engine. The Brits always do things backward, so the BSA shifts on the right and breaks on the left, just the opposite of a Harley. The bike had a kick start, and if it wasn't ridden often enough, it got cold-blooded and wouldn't start. I won a trophy in a bike show for the antique class, but soon realized I wanted something that wasn't as high maintenance. I hauled it to an antique bike swap meet held each year in Davenport at their fair grounds on Labor Day week end. I just parked it and waited for someone to ask me about it. I sold it for more than I had paid and then spent the night there to see the antique cycle races on a half mile dirt track. These are not only old bikes, but they are ridden by antique riders as well. The bikes were as old as 1919 vintage, and some of the riders were in their sixties and seventies. These guys still knew how to ride, sliding their foot on the corners and going flat out on the straight-a-ways.

I had seen a 1994 Harley Davidson Fat Boy around town and really liked it. It was owned by Don Batt, and he had taken really good care of it. He was going to buy a later model Road King and had put the Fat Boy up for sale. I struck a deal and bought it, much to Nancy's disappointment. If you haven't gathered, she is not a big motorcycle fan. I think my fascination with cycles began with a feeling I used to get riding horse. It is a feeling of freedom with the wind in your face that is hard to describe to a non-rider. I was a little apprehensive riding a big bike as it was the first one like that I had ever been on. There really isn't a lot of difference other than the weight; you don't want to tip it over because it weighs seven hundred pounds. I was in Ames once at a ride in, and we took a short ride through town when at a stop sign I turned around to see if Danny was behind me, and my bad knee buckled and the bike went down. It was embarrassing and several guys helped me get it vertical again. Dan wanted to know if I was going to order training wheels.

In 1992 Kirke Quinn and I went on a road trip to Sturgis, South Dakota. We cheated, though, and drove out in a pickup truck with the bikes on a trailer behind. We stopped at the famous Wall Drug on the way out for a bite to eat and see what the two hundred billboards were about before we got to Wall. Because it was August and it was hot, we were dressed in tennis shorts when we went in to eat. This was not customary motorcycle garb, and we looked a little out of place. Kirke and I were sitting near a burley biker that was obviously riding who was lathered with "ink" and had his head shaved. Kirke, trying to be funny says, "Do you think anyone will know we're gay?" Real funny, Kirke!

Sturgis is an experience to behold. There must be some two hundred thousand bikers in the area at any one time. It would be easier to tell you what you don't see than what you do. The main street of the town of Sturgis is lined from one end to the other with bikes of all descriptions. You had better remember where you park, or you could spend a long time looking for your cycle. I had just traded for an anniversary Fat Boy, so it was as new a bike as you could get. It was black with a special anniversary package called the gold key package. Kirke had a Road King, so we looked the part once we got our "biker clothes" on and the bikes off the trailer. We stayed with Mike McFarland and his wife and paid them for letting us sleep in their basement.

I had been to the Black Hills as a kid with my parents and had forgotten how pretty it is. We rode to see Mount Rushmore, Custer National Park, with buffalo and all. We rode to Deadwood and saw the casinos and had a good time. Kirke doesn't have a very long attention span, so we didn't stay any one place too long. We rode into Wyoming and saw Devils Tower one day and then started the twelve-hour drive home on our third day there.

Jim and Kirke Quinn posing with the presidents at Mt. Rushmore
and near the Sturgus Motorcycle Ralley 2002

I don't take very long trips on my cycle because Nancy and I like to do things together, and she doesn't like to ride. She once rode to Ames with me and had her legs so tight to the bike that the muffler burnt her rubber heels on her boots. She rode one other time with me and a group to a dance in Stratford a few miles north of Boone. When she got off the back of my bike and took her helmet off, the first person she saw was one of her students, who turned to her mother and said "Look, it's my teacher, Mrs. Grabau, Mom."

In 2003 Harley Davidson celebrated their one-hundredth anniversary. They had a big party in Milwaukee, and I thought it would be a fun destination ride. I went as a lone wolf and took off in the afternoon planning to ride about half way that evening. I rode to Monroe, Wisconsin, and spent the night there. The next day I rode into Milwaukee to see the gathering. They had all kinds of things going on right next to Lake Michigan, and the weather was beautiful. I didn't stick around for the bands like Stephenwolf that played that night because, one, I didn't have a ticket, and two, I didn't want to get caught in all the after party traffic on my motorcycle late at night. I rode instead to Lake Geneva and stayed with Nancy's cousin, Bob Couffer, and his wife, Jeanne. I had bought a funny dew rag with long hair coming out the back and traded my helmet for the dew rag when I got to their home. We all had a good laugh, and I took them out to dinner.

I rode home the next day, and Nancy had been so worried about my ride, she had a case of the shingles. Riding can be dangerous, but I do think it makes a person a very defensive driver because you always have to watch what the other drivers are going to do. If you tie, you lose!

In 2008 I traded my Fat Boy for a Soft Tail Deluxe. It is a throw-back style bike that has white walls and spoke wheels and is about the same size as a Fat Boy. The bike is two-tone black and blue, and I kept the same saddle bags I had on my Fat Boy. I really do enjoy riding, but don't get to do it as much as I like. In the summer I sometimes ride it to check on jobs as an excuse to give it some exercise.

LEADERSHIP

IN HIGH SCHOOL the yearbook staff put a saying by each senior picture. Some of them were humorous, some serious, and some had more truth than we wanted to know. Mine said, James Grabau: "Thou has seen nothing yet." When I reflect on my high school career, it was very true. I was a classic underachiever. I think someone saw potential, but it was very much unrealized. I was nominated for president of the student council and wasn't able to run because my grades were too poor. It was one of the more embarrassing moments of my life. It may have woken me up though, and I have spent a great deal of my life trying to contribute in some way to the betterment of whatever I am involved in.

In junior college I ran for president of The Young Republicans and was elected. I wasn't so much motivated by politics as I thought it could be a fun social outlet. We recruited everyone we could, and told them to join because we have great parties, trips, etc. The Young Republicans club from Boone JC had the largest percentage of our enrollment for the school of all the colleges in the state. We won an award for that at the state convention. The Republicans didn't win the election for president that year; our candidate was Barry Goldwater. I was most impressed by a speaker that gave the keynote speech at the national convention by the name of Ronald Reagan.

I did better grade wise at the JC and transferred to Texas Christian University after getting my AA Degree from Boone Junior College. My friend, Fritz Westfall, invited me down for a weekend in the spring of my sophomore year. It was still winter in Iowa, and I went water skiing in Fort Worth, so the decision was made.

There have been several Boone students that have graduated from TCU over the years. Dick Hamilton was one of the first followed by Sue Caldwell, Fritz Westfall, me, and another friend of mine, John Johnson. I went through rush and ended up pledging Delta Tau Delta fraternity. Fritz was affiliated with the Phi Delts, which was another good house, but I felt I fit in with the Delts, so that's what I did.

We had a pledge class of about twenty-three guys, and most of them were freshman. At our first meeting I was nominated to be president of my pledge class and was elected. I remember running my first meeting and making some mistakes in procedure and needing to read up on "Robert's Rules of Order," which I did. When you mess up or make a mistake, it can be a good thing if it motivates you to become better. We had some great bonding experiences, but only nine of our pledge class made good enough grades to become actives. I was one that made it, thank goodness. I matured in some of my leadership skills and found out it's not easy being at the front of even a pledge class. Sometimes you have to be the peacekeeper and sometimes the babysitter, but your main goal is to keep the group working together. We had a picture taken of our pledge class, I guess because we thought we were so good looking, and gave it to the chapter to hang in a prestigious spot. They laughed out loud, gave it back, and said they didn't want any pictures of a pledge class hanging anywhere but the "john"!

My senior year the Viet Nam war was in full swing, and I knew I would get drafted the moment I graduated, so I joined the Marine Corps Reserve in Fort Worth, so as to have some control of my destiny. I didn't realize it at the time, but this was a very important part of my education. I became disciplined and also learned more about leadership even though I was being told what to do twenty-four seven. I was a platoon leader, and had I gone to war, those men would have depended on me to do the right thing. I also gained a deep respect for those who have gone to war to preserve the wonderful freedoms we enjoy in America.

When I completed my active duty, I went back to finish college and graduated in 1968. Nancy and I moved back to Boone, and I got involved in the Boone Jaycees. Back then it was the best organization to get to know young people and also make a contribution to the community. I had seen men that I looked up to participate in the Jaycees when I was in junior college. These included Lloyd Courter, Paul Stark, Dave Boehm, and Mike Newbold, as well as many others. I looked to these men as mentors that I wanted to learn from and learn from their success. I became an officer and participated in many of their activities from when I was twenty-two until I was thirty-five, the cut-off age back then for Jaycees. I ran for president of the chapter one year and lost in a close election to Dale Points. I served as one of his vice presidents and gained more experience.

I was asked to serve on the Board of the Chamber of Commerce. James Nash was the president, and it was during those years that Pufferbilly Days was born. We wanted to have a community celebration, and little by little, it developed into a big deal. I was elected president of the board in 1979. I had become much more comfortable in front of a group and tried to run an efficient meeting. I asked Denny McFarland and Rick LePera to co-chair Pufferbilly Days, and they agreed, if they could do it their way. I had been a day chair a couple of years earlier and hadn't done that great of a job, looking back. Denny and Rick did a great job, and I think it was the first year the celebration really took off. They started the button idea to raise money and also the beer tent, which was successful, but very small compared to a few years later.

My dad thought I should become involved in the Industrial Development Corporation, and I was elected to the board of that organization in the early eighties. It was a good place to keep an eye on what proactive things are going on to sustain or attract new industry to Boone. In a small town everyone gets to spend time in the barrel, so I was elected president of that group for a few years.

In 1985 I was nominated and elected to the Board of The Master Builders of Iowa. It was a three-year term back then unless you became president, and then you served four. I should have learned that when you open your mouth too often, you find yourself running the meeting in a year or two, and I was elected president of the MBI in 1987. My dad had served on the board many years before, and I always thought of the group as what Ken Lewis said to me once, "The best of the best." I was flattered to be on the board and that they trusted me to be its president. It wasn't an easy year as we had some major challenges but also a good staff that made us look good. We won "Chapter of The Year/President of The Year Award" that year thanks to the great support from a partnership of members and staff. Jim Ryan was our executive VP then and deserves much of the credit for this award given to only one chapter from all of the states. I do have good timing and was in the right place at the right time. One sad note was that my dad died in August of 1987, and he is still missed in my life. He was eighty years old. My mother lived another thirteen years and died at the age of ninety-three. Both of my parents were a major influence on my life.

I became a director of Hawkeye Savings and Loan in about 1985 and served until we sold the bank to Commercial Federal about ten years later. The board members I first joined the board with included; Lloyd Courter, Paul Stark, Reinhold Josephson, George Peterson and John Peterson. Board members that joined the board later included; Stan Moffitt, John Walker, Bernie Saggau, Cay Herrald and Sally Courter. I was very privlidged to be in such an accomplished group. It was great experience for me to see how a financial institution is run and participate in some major decisions. Hawkeye became the very first Stock Savings and Loan in Iowa. It was not a sure deal because there were a bunch of financial institutions that went under all over the country. I purchased stock, and it turned out to be the best investment I ever made. I only wish I had bought more.

The Boone Industrial Development Corporation had been formed as a for profit entity in the fifties because they thought it would be easier to sell stock in the organization. This made it difficult for the corporation to do any joint ventures with the city and the county. In the early nineties we started a new group to do industrial development called "Boone's Future." I suggested the name because I thought people would want to invest in Boone's Future. The group now receives support from the major financial institutions as well as the city, county, and many businesses throughout the community. I took my turn in that barrel in 1993.

I have been a member of Trinity Lutheran Church since I was born, which is more than a few years ago. Nancy and I were youth group leaders when our kids were very young. I served as stewardship chairman and later as an elder, all of which were very worthwhile. I became chairman of the congregation in 2005 and served until 2009. The toughest thing about a church position is that the church is always in need of more money. It is hard to be proactive when you don't have the funds. The church has always been a central part of my life and my family's. There are times when I could set a better example to others, and that's when I most appreciate "grace."

Dick Johnson and I have given a class on our experiences in leadership positions for the MBI "Eye On The Future" course they have started to develop future leaders in the organization. I have several points I try to convey to the class, and these are a few: Being a leader is a journey, not a destination. Good leaders have several qualities, and they include: being able to communicate, able and willing to listen, able to admit mistakes and learn from them, able to be an eternal optimist and able to convey this to others, able to have a sense of humor, able to run a meeting and keep it on task, and finally, able to have balance in your life, including spiritual, work, family, and recreation. I also think leaders should: 1. Have goals and write them down, 2. Treat setbacks as challenges and grow from them, 3. Keep yourself under control, 4. Be able to say no when you are not capable or don't have the time to serve, 5. Give others the opportunity to contribute and also lead, 6. Don't lead for the glory, 7. Finally, give others the credit. In any leadership position I have served, I always look back and see where I could have done a better job. I thank all those who gave me a chance to be involved in some great organizations.

ADVENTURE

I FEEL MOST of life has been an adventure. There are a couple of stories that were out of my comfort zone that were what I call "adventures." When I was a junior in college, and my first year at TCU, I had a fraternity brother that was called "Crash" McKinley. He was given this handle because the first time he sky dived, he broke his ankle. He asked if anyone else in the fraternity wanted to learn to sky dive. Wilson Craigie, Richard Rachal, and I thought it would be fun, so we went with him to see what it involved. The sky diving club did their jumping in Cedar Hill, a small town near Dallas. We were really excited when we saw the Cessna Plane take off and climb to five thousand feet or so for the diver's first jump, a thirty-second delay. We could hear the plane cut its engine, and the divers were out the door of the plane and falling. They have an altimeter and a stop watch to tell them when to pull the rip cord. When they approach thirty seconds, they pull their chute, a canopy goes up, and they drift to earth. What's not to like about that?

Wilson Craigie and Jim before our first sky diving experience at Cedar Hill, Texas

We signed the release forms, paid our instruction fee, and were enrolled in a pre-jump class. It met in the evening, and we were taught all the nomenclature of the chute, how we would get out of the plane and into position on the plane's wing strut, how to arch our back after we let go, and how to pull our dummy rip cord on our first few jumps. We were given a log book to record our jumps and told that if we lose the rip cord handle, we had to buy a keg for the club. Our first jump was to be Saturday afternoon at the Cedar Hill jump site. We arrived early to get our gear on and prepare for the first and hopefully not our last jump. I had to borrow a jump suit and a helmet as well as the chute. I'm not sure what the helmet was for because if the chute didn't open, that helmet wasn't going to do much good. The plane we would be jumping out of had only one seat in it, and that was the pilot's. There was no door on the right side of the plane for easy exit. The pilot thought it was funny to take off and then roll the plane, so whoever was sitting by the door opening would almost fall out.

I like to do some adventurous things, but I do have inward fear. I was beginning to get sweaty palms as we climbed into the plane. They told us when we were next to climb out the door and put one foot on the wing strut and the other on the plane's wheel. That was another thing the pilot thought was funny when he would not lock the break, so when you put your foot on the wheel, it would turn, and you would almost fall right then. The guy had a warped sense of humor. We would jump with a static line a little like they do in the military. A static line is connected to your rip cord and a hook on the plane. When you jump free from the plane, it pulls your rip cord, and your chute opens, you hope. I was in the front seat, so I had to go first. The plane climbed to an elevation of three thousand feet, and that is where beginners do their first jump. I was told to climb out and get in position. My palms were really wet now, and my brain was saying to me, "Why would anyone jump out of a perfectly good plane?" I was now in position, and they cut the engine and said go! They had to tell me twice because my fingers didn't want to let go. I finally let go and looked down to pull my dummy rip cord. By just looking down for a split second, I had done a flip, and then I felt the jerk of my shoot opening. What a thrill and relief when you look up and see the canopy of your chute full of air as you drift towards earth. It is very serene up there, and you can hear voices from a long ways away.

I was enjoying this "sky diving" now and looking for a place to land. We jumped with a canopy type chute, and not the air foil type they use today. We had a toggle line on each side. I was told that as I got close to the ground to pull one of the lines and the chute would turn, preventing the wind from moving me forward, and I would come straight down. I saw a row of trees along a fence line with a plowed field just on the other side. I thought what a great place to land in the nice soft dirt. I pulled on the line just as I was passing over the tree line thinking I would drift a short ways into the plowed field. I didn't realize that once you pull the cord, it is like putting on the brakes, and I came straight down, and the first thing I felt was the top tree limbs. I was fortunate not to get hurt, but it didn't help the chute that I had borrowed any.

Jim trying to get chute out of a tree after first jump

I can't remember if was the same day or a week or two later, we were walking back from where we had landed when we looked up to see a jumper named Joe Nyokes, one of the instructors with over four hundred jumps, doing a thirty-second delay when his chute was causing him to spin. Joe jumped with a chute called a Para-commander that has lines that run up the middle for more control when doing competitive jumps. If the lines get tangled, they can cause the chute to spin, or what is called a "May West." Joe had to decide in midair if he thought he could land or go to his reserve. It was no more than a split second, and Joe reached up and pinched his cape wells that released his main chute. He then pulled his reserve rip cord and a smaller emergency chute was deployed. He was a big guy, so he hit a little harder than he would have liked, but we were all relieved that he made it down safely.

I made the mistake of telling my parents of my new hobby. They weren't too thrilled, and I was informed that if I continued that the rest of my schooling would be on my own! I had made just four jumps to this point. It usually takes five jumps to become stable, so they trust you to do some jump and pulls. You work up to fifteen-second delays and then thirty. Some good jumpers do sixty-second delays, but with our small plane, it takes forever to get to twelve thousand feet, the height required for that long of delay. Depending on his form, a diver falls at about 120 feet per second. A diver falls some 9000 feet in sixty seconds.

Today the equipment is more sophisticated, and the first jumps are tandem with an instructor. My daughter, Alison, likes to "one up" me on most things, so she did a tandem dive that was a minute delay. I think she was braver her first time than I was, and she enjoyed it more. She also didn't land in a tree, but did get her jump caught on video. I see divers jump near Boone all the time because the Iowa State Dive Club uses the Boone Airport for their base. Well, who knows, maybe I can celebrate birthdays like George Bush Sr. and jump again with a little more freefall.

SPIRITUAL

I WAS RAISED in the Missouri Lutheran Church, which to some is like religious boot camp. I never felt that way and remain in the same church today. Lutherans take the Bible very literally and believe it is the inspired word of God. There are some parts of the Bible that are very difficult to understand. It is my belief that we believe by faith and not reason when we don't understand everything we read. My parents took us to church every Sunday and also had us in Sunday school class. I believe that a person's spiritual being is just as important as their physical or mental being. I also believe that I am a sinner and that the grace of God as given by his son Jesus Christ is my only way to eternal life.

My confirmation class with Pastor Seltz
at Trinity Lutheran Church, Boone, Iowa

I do not always live the exemplary life that I should as a Christian. I do feel the church has always been a very important part of my total life. I hope that if nothing else, I passed this on to my children and grandchildren. I only went one year to the Trinity Lutheran School, but Nancy and I did send both of our children to it for their first eight years. They got a good education and a spiritual background that will stay with them for life.

When I was in about sixth grade, I had some fainting spells. I was in church and standing up during the prayer when I felt this weird, light-headed feeling that would precede my passing out. I fell and hit my head on the pew in front of me and let out a loud scream. My dad took me out for fresh air, and Pastor Seltz thought someone had fallen out of the balcony. I got over these except for that time I fainted at a fellow Marine's wedding when I was his best man. It was a Catholic wedding, and we Lutherans aren't used to kneeling that long!

My philosophy has always been to strive for balance in your life between work, activities, mental and physical, family, and spiritual. If you can keep these in a fairly close balance, your chance at happiness is much more likely. I was talking to a classmate at a reunion and told him that there are things that I wish I had done better as I look back at my life, but sometimes our failures create the ground work for future success. I think God places challenges in front of us that make us better people from going through a few rough times.

I often feel like Forrest Gump in that so many good things happened to me, I was just in the right place at the right time. I am sure that I didn't deserve most of my blessings and hope that I am always grateful for them. The things I value most are the relationships that I have had with friends and family, and all the good memories they bring to mind. "Say, that reminds me of a story." I now have four grandchildren. Sam is my eldest at eight, followed by Sophie who is six, and then William who is twenty-two months. These are all Grabaus with parents Ryan and Andrea. Dr. Ben and Alison Pomerantz have a little girl named Morgan who is ten months. I love them all, and there is no greater feeling than having a grandchild call you "Papa." This truly has been "a wonderful life."

Family in front of Lake Geneva, Wisconsin from left Dr Ben and Alison
Pomerantz, Grammy and Papa, Sophie, Andrea, Sam and Ryan Grabau

Sam, Grammy, Morgan, Sophie, Papa and William